Dear Parents and Educators,

Thank you for purchasing this excellent teaching resource! This resource was created especially for elementary students to learn individually or while working with peers as the teacher presents each topic. The workbook can be used in the classroom or as part of a homeschooling program. Multiple subjects are embedded in the lessons, such as personal hygiene, introduction to kingdoms, human body systems and Earth Science. The embedded laboratories will allow the student to learn new topics while practicing basic skills.

This resource was created to promote scientific investigation, Character Development and Bible Exploration. The Vision of Azalea Park Church: *To encourage the spiritual, social and academic development of all children.*

Azalea Park Church Mission: *To Continue the Teaching Ministry of Jesus Christ.*

**www.AzaleaParkChurch.Org**

All rights reserved, including the right to reproduce this workbook or portions. For information, address the publisher, A & W Publishing, LLC
5725 Dahlia Dr. Orlando, Fl 32807

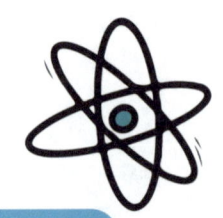

NAME:_____

TEACHER: _____

GRADE: _____

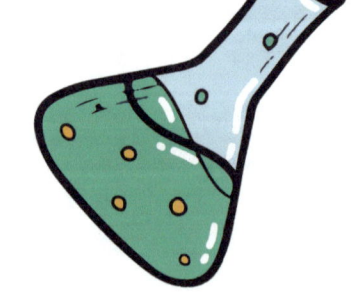

# CONTENT OVERVIEW

## SUGGESTIONS

This resource can be used along a formal science curriculum for enhancement since it provides many learning opportunities for the student.

It may be used as part of a homeschooling program to introduce general essential science concepts for young children.

The material is divided in four quarters and by the branches of science such as, anatomy, botany, life science, chemistry and earth science.

# Table of Content
# Unit 1

| Topic | Page |
|---|---|
| Safety is all about responsibility | 6-8 |
| Experiment: We are all Alike | 9 |
| Healthy Habits | 10-12 |
| Taking Care of Your Brain | 13-15 |
| Parts of the Body | 16-18 |
| The Five Senses | 19-29 |
| Dental Hygiene | 30-31 |
| Human Body Organs and Systems | 32-40 |
| Food Chain Project | |

# Table of Content Unit 2

| Topic | Page |
|---|---|
| The Plant World | 44-45 |
| Kingdoms | 46 |
| Biodiversity | 47-53 |
| Photosynthesis | 54-62 |
| Animal Cell | 63-64 |
| Sorting Plants and Animals | 65-68 |
| Vertebrates and Invertebrates | 69-71 |
| Insects | 72-75 |
| Science Project: Butterfly Cycle | 76 |

# Table of Content Unit 3

| Topic | Page |
|---|---|
| Scientific Method | 80-83 |
| States of Matter | 84-89 |
| Experiment: Sin is like a Thread | 90 |
| Experiment: Comparing sunflower and bean seeds | 91-95 |
| Properties of Matter | 96-97 |
| Energy Types | 98 |
|  |  |
|  |  |

# Table of Content Unit 4

| Topic | Page |
|---|---|
| Bodies of Water | 104 |
| Continents and Oceans | 106-107 |
| Water Cycle | 108 |
| Experiment: Sink or Float predictions | 109 |
| Layers of the Earth' Atmosphere | 110 |
| Project: Solar System Model | 111-121 |
| Recycling is Everyone's Responsibility | 122-123 |
| Natural Disasters | 124-127 |
| Save the Earth | 128-135 |
| Teacher Resources & Answer Keys | 136 |

# All About Me!

Name:

I am

years old

I like...

My family picture

My favorite activities are
- 
- 
- 

My favorite subjects are
- 
- 
- 

I'm really good at

My favorite foods are

# Table of Content
# Unit 1

| Topic | Page |
|---|---|
| Safety is all about responsibility | 6-8 |
| Experiment: We are all Alike | 9 |
| Healthy Habits | 10-12 |
| Taking Care of Your Brain | 13-15 |
| Parts of the Body | 16-18 |
| The Five Senses | 19-29 |
| Dental Hygiene | 30-31 |
| Human Body Organs and Systems | 32-40 |
| Food Chain Project | |

# My Body at Work

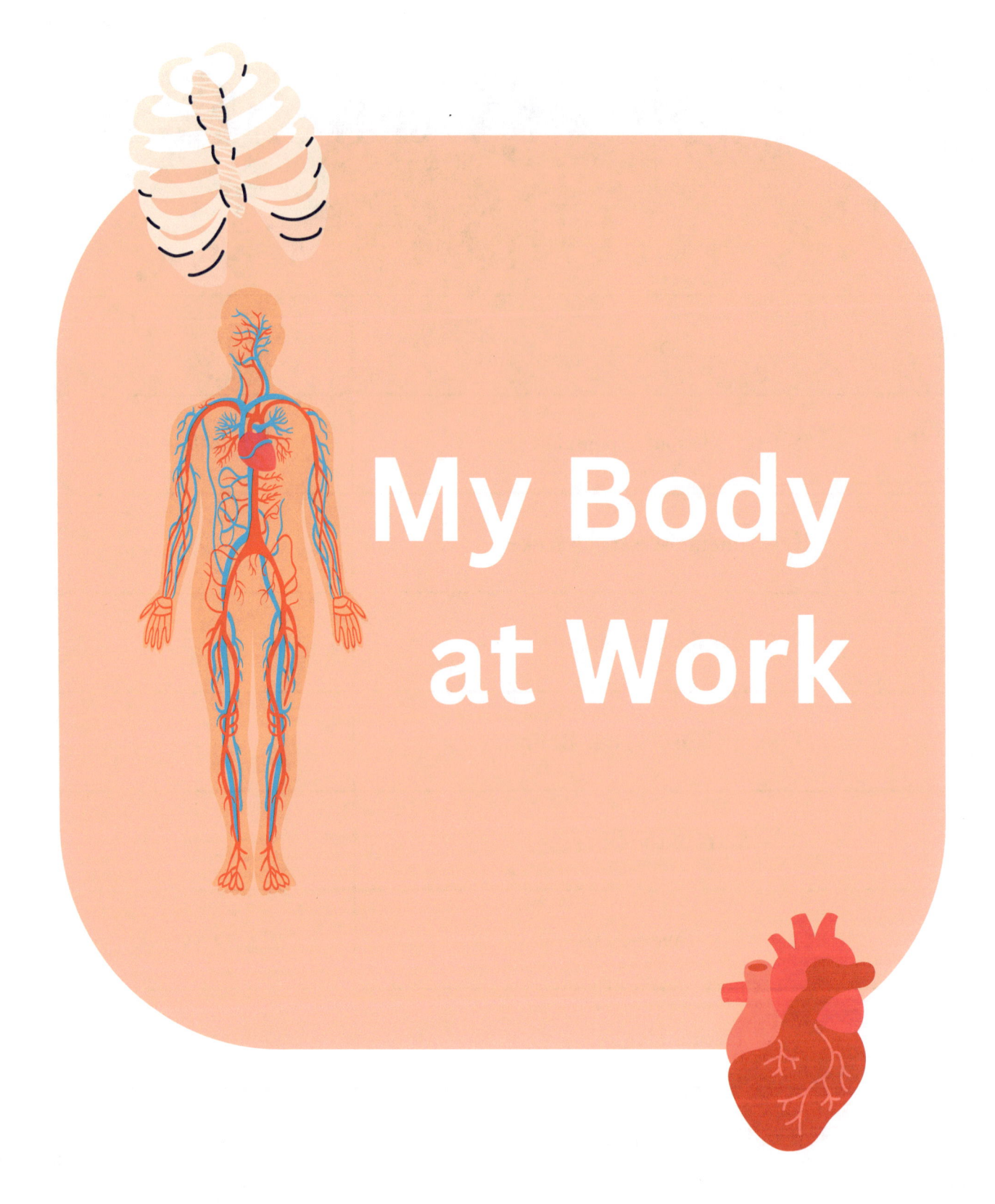

# CAUTION

## WORK WITH CARE!

# SAFETY SAVES LIVES

## Safety Tips:

- Know the locations of laboratory safety equipment, and fire extinguishers (in the hallways)

- Avoid skin and eye contact with chemicals

# Science Safety is all about Responsibility

The Bible has a lot to say about taking responsibility for our actions.

Luke 10:30 -37 We are to be responsible for the way we act toward others.
1 Timothy 5:8 We are responsible for the way we treat our families.
2 Timothy 2:15 We are responsible to study God's Word.

we are also responsible for the way we treat our school resources. lett uscreate some safety rules for our science class. Together.

## *Our Classroom Rules:*

1.

2.

3.

4.

5.

# Science Experiment: We are all Alike

We all live on planet Earth; it is our home. Make new friends, even if they act or look different, inside we are all the same.

Complete the next page first before we start

**Materials:**

1 white egg
1 brown egg
1 quail egg

Draw each egg on the boxes below
What do you think the eggs look like on the inside?
With the help of an adult crack each egg and draw what they look like inside

| The white Egg looks like this... | The brown Egg looks like this... | The Quail Egg looks like this... |
|---|---|---|
|  |  |  |

Crack open the eggs. Draw what you see in the spaces provided.

| White Egg. | Brown Egg. | Quail |
|---|---|---|
|  |  |  |

# Healthy Habits

| | | |
|---|---|---|
| wash your hands | brush your teeth | take a shower |
| eat healthy foods | drink plenty of water | exercise |
| get enough sleep | brush your hair | trim your nails |

# Practice Healthy Habits

| | | |
|---|---|---|
| Wash your hands | Brush your teeth | Have a bath or shower |
| Do exercise | Eat healthy food | Drink plenty of water |
| Go to bed early | Sleep 8 or more hours | Spend time with the people you love |
| Practice kindness and gratitude | Take time to relax and rest | Read and learn new things |

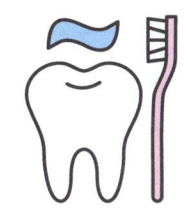

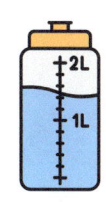

# Summarize what you've learned about Healthy Habits

Date:

Topic:

# Taking Care of Your Brain

Mental Health means celebrating yourself and honoring who you are. To be nice to yourself is to speak positively about you and to accept compliments from others.

Your brain can stay healthy when you think more positively. Here are some ways you can take better care of your brain.

Step 1: Think positive thoughts
Step 2: Take care of yourself. ...
Step 3: Prioritize what's important. ...
Step 4: Change how you think about you
Step 5: Notice the good things. ...

Can you think of one good thing about YOU?

I can do all things through Christ which strengthens me. Philippians 4:13

# Be kind to your mind
Color the picture

## Mental Health Matters

# I am Calm

Color the picture

## Mental Health Matters

# PARTS OF THE BODY

Label the body parts in this diagram.

**WORD BANK**

eye

chest    foot    hand    eyebrow    Private Part

stomach    hair    mouth    ear    shoulder

# SCIENCE RESEARCH REPORT

**TOPIC: THE ANIMAL CELL**  Key Points:

_____

_____

_____

_____

Summary:

_____

_____

_____

_____

_____

_____

_____

_____

_____

# NEW VOCABULARY

What new words have you learned as you do your research? Write them below.

| WORD | MEANING | PICTURE |
|---|---|---|
|  |  |  |
|  |  |  |
|  |  |  |

# MY FIVE SENSES

Match the words on the left to its picture on the right.

hear •

sight •

taste •

smell •

touch •

# FIVE SENSES

Fill in the blanks with the words in the box.

hear
see
smell
taste
touch

I ..................

I ..................

I ..................

I ..................

I ..................

# SENSE OF SIGHT

Describe different things you might see throughout the day

My favorite sight is _____

because _____

# PARTS OF THE EYE

**Fill in the blanks with the words in the box.**

> optic nerve / choroid / sclera
> lens / iris / cornea / retina / pupil

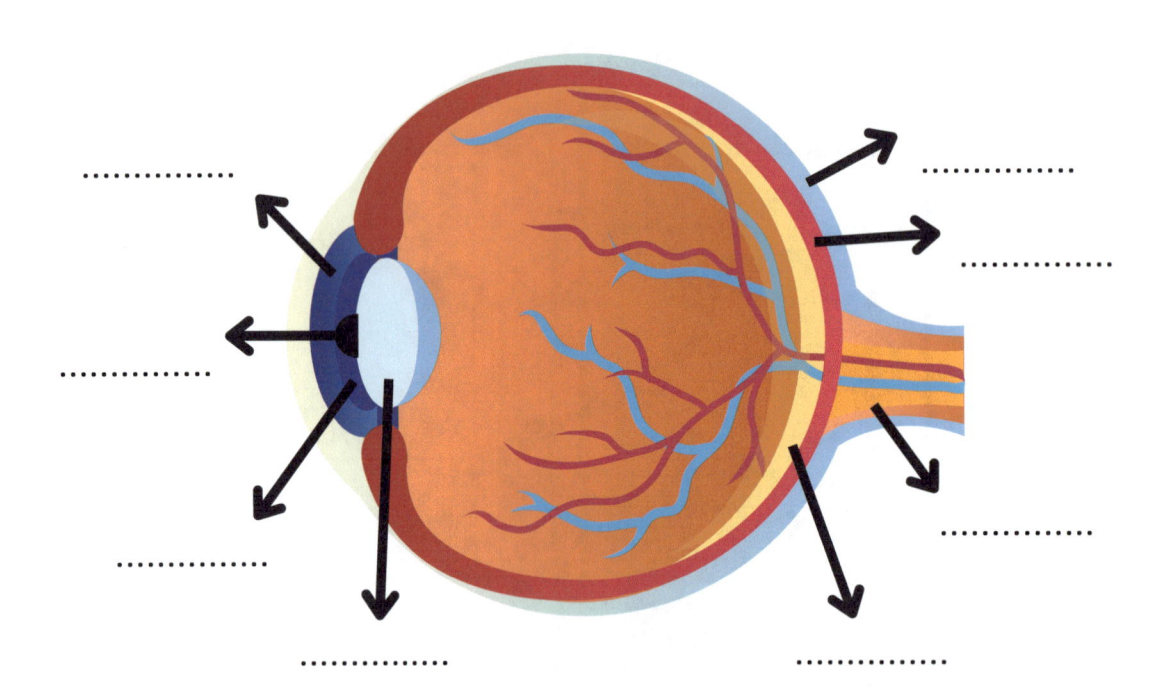

**Fill in the blanks with some words in the box above.**

1- The coloured circular part of that eye that surrounds the black pupil is ..............

2- .............. is the transparent covering of the eye that protects the front of it.

3- .............. is the area at the back of the eye that receives light and sends pictures of what the eye sees to the brain.

4- The circular blackarea in the centre of an eye is ..............

5- .............. is the group of nerve fibres that pass signals from the retina at the back of each eye to the brain.

# SCIENCE RESEARCH: HUMAN EYE

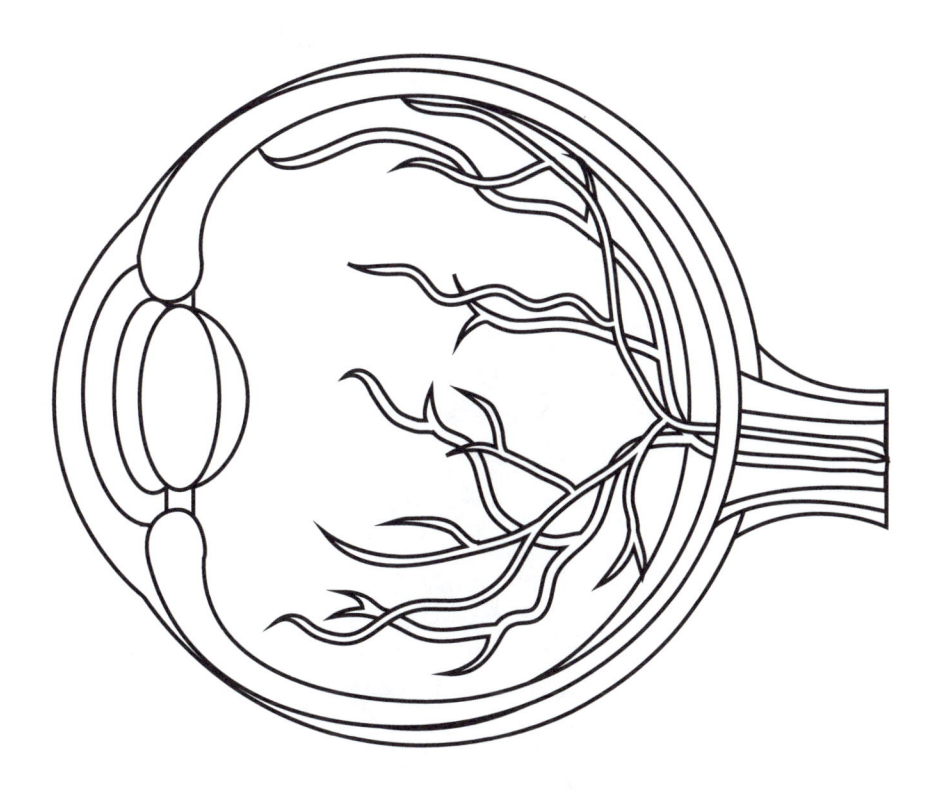

Look at the illustration of the human eye. Label its parts and describe the function of each part.

_____
_____
_____
_____
_____

# 4 Fruits that are Healthy For Your Eyes

Avocado

Carrot

Blueberries

Pitaya

# SENSE OF SOUND

Describe different sounds you might hear throughout the day

My favourite sound is _____

because _____

# SCIENCE RESEARCH REPORT

**TOPIC: HUMAN EAR**

Key Points:

_____

_____

_____

_____

Summary:

_____

_____

_____

_____

_____

_____

_____

_____

_____

# SENSE OF TOUCH

Describe different things you might touch throughout the day, and what they feel like

My favourite texture is _____

because _____

# SENSE OF
# SMELL

Describe different things you might smell throughout the day

My favourite scent is _____

because _____

# SENSE OF
# TASTE

Describe different things you might taste throughout the day

My favourite taste is _____

because _____

# TYPES OF TEETH

Write the words under the pictures.

**Incisor / Canine / Premolar / Molar**

....................  ....................  ....................  ....................

How many teeth have you got?
_____

How often do you brush your teeth?
_____

What else do you need to do to
keep your teeth clean and healthy?
_____
_____
_____
_____

# MY TEETH

Draw and write the things you use to clean your teeth.

How often do you brush your teeth?

I brush my teeth ..............................................

How many teeth have you got?

I've got .............. teeth.

Number of teeth you've lost:

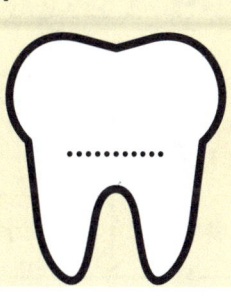

# Human Body Internal Organs

Look at the pictures and circle the correct words

| | | | |
|---|---|---|---|
| (brain) | Heart / Brain | (heart) | Stomach / Heart |
| (lungs) | Liver / Lungs | (pancreas) | Pancreas / Ureter |
| (intestine) | Intestine / Trachea | (kidneys) | Lungs / Kidneys |
| (bladder) | Bladder / Spleen | (stomach) | Stomach / Brain |
| (liver) | Liver / Stomach | (kidney) | Bladder / Spleen |

# Human Body Internal Organs
Look at the pictures and circle the correct words

| What is the job of this organ? | What is the job of this organ? |
|---|---|
| What is the job of this organ? | What is the job of this organ? |
| What is the job of this organ? | What is the job of this organ? |
| What is the job of this organ? | What is the job of this organ? |
| What is the job of this organ? | What is the job of this organ? |

GRADE: _____ Out of _____

# DIGESTIVE SYSTEM

Fill in the blanks with the words in the box.

| small intestine / large intestine / rectum / appendix stomach / liver / pancreas / oesophagus / gallbladder |

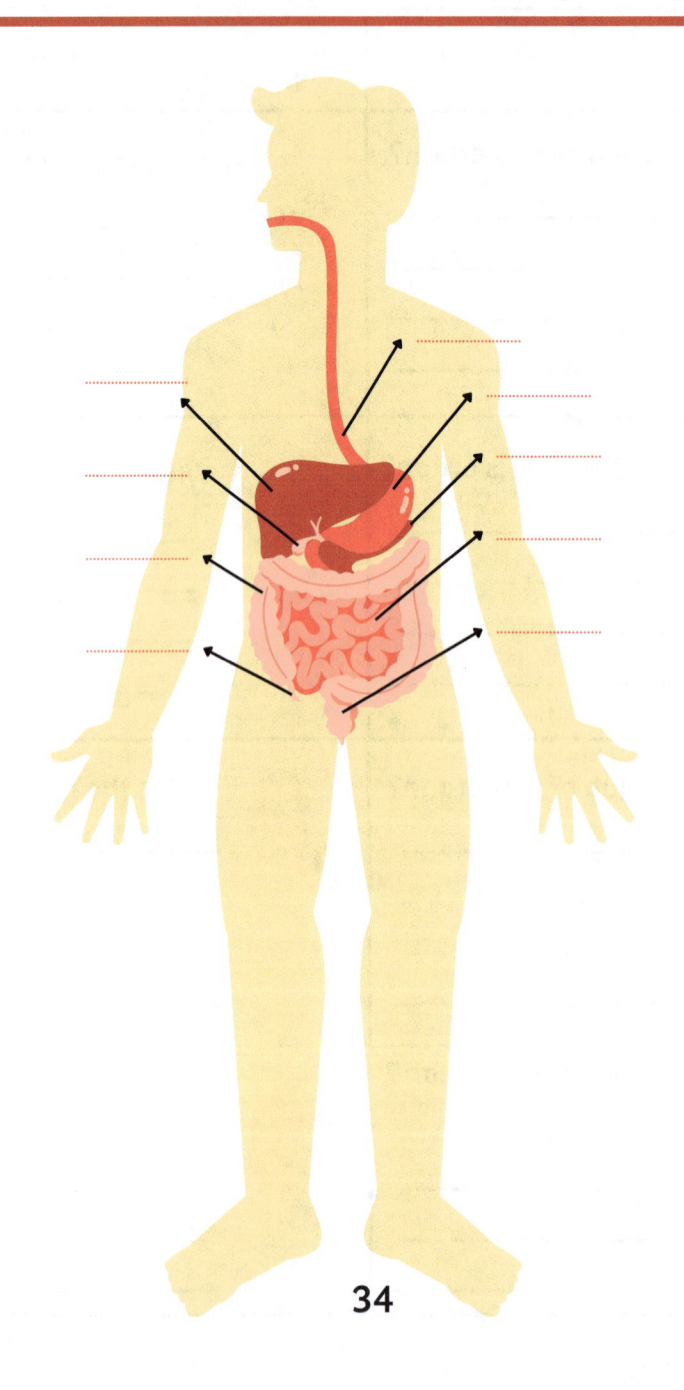

# RESPIRATORY SYSTEM

Fill in the blanks with the words in the box.

> nasal cavity / left lung / larynx / oral cavity
> right lung / bronchi / trachea / bronchioles / pharynx

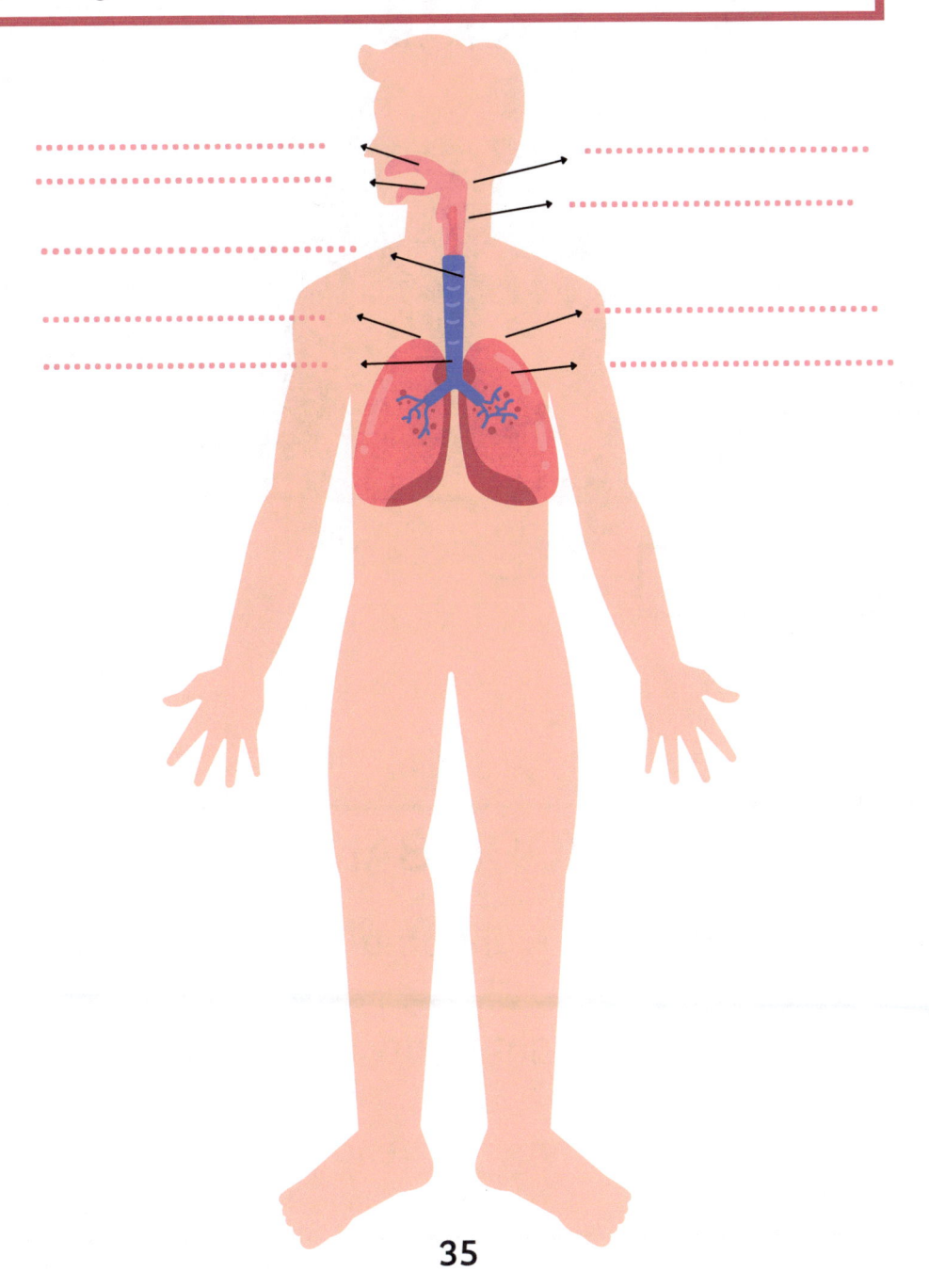

GRADE: _____ Out of _____

# THE HUMAN HEART

Label the different parts of the heart and write the correct answer in the box provided.

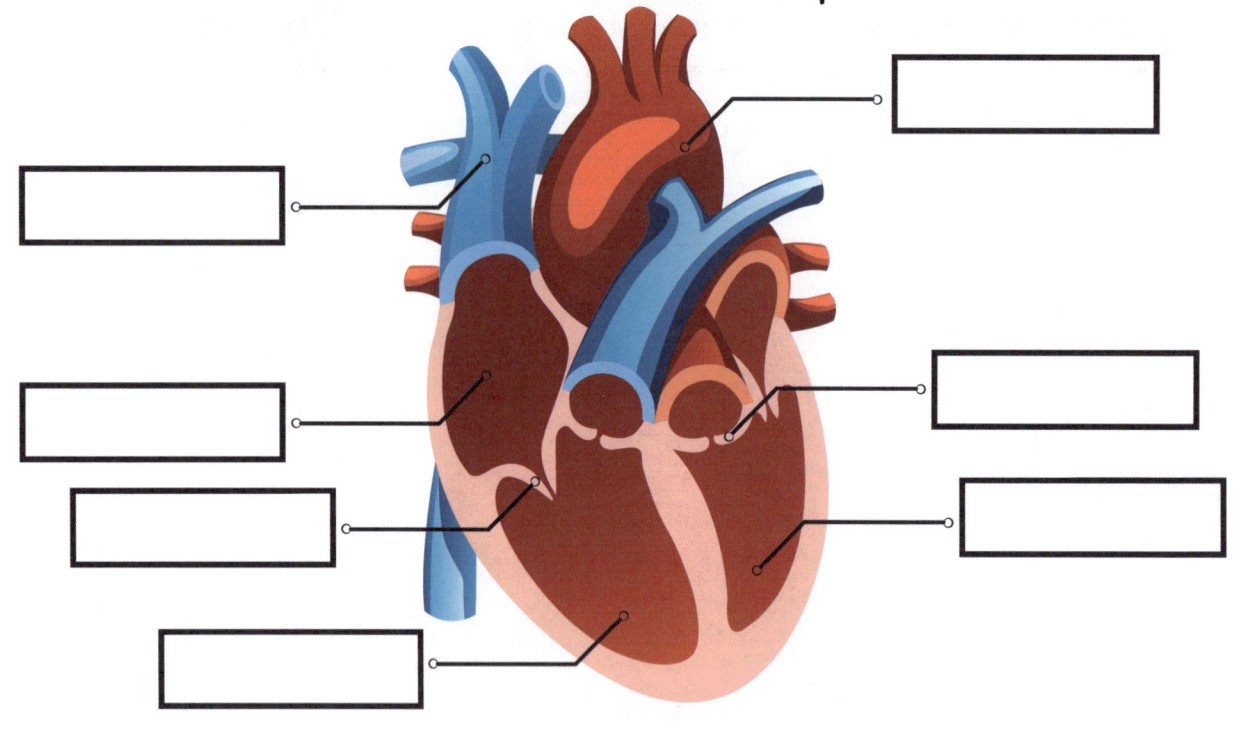

## WORD BANK

| Left ventricle | Right atria | Aorta |
| Mitral valve | Right ventricle | Tricuspid valve |
| | Superior vena cava | |

36

GRADE: _____ Out of _____

# The Skeletal System

Look at the pictures and circle the correct words

| | | | |
|---|---|---|---|
| | Pelvis / Vertebrae | | Jaws / Ribs |
| | Patella / Femur | | Fibula / Skull |
| | Spine / Pelvis | | Tarsals / Tibia |
| | Scapula / Humerus | | Metacarpals / Metatarsals |
| | Mandible / Skull | | Sternum / Phalanges |

39

# The Skeletal System

Label the bones in the body using the words at the bottom of the page

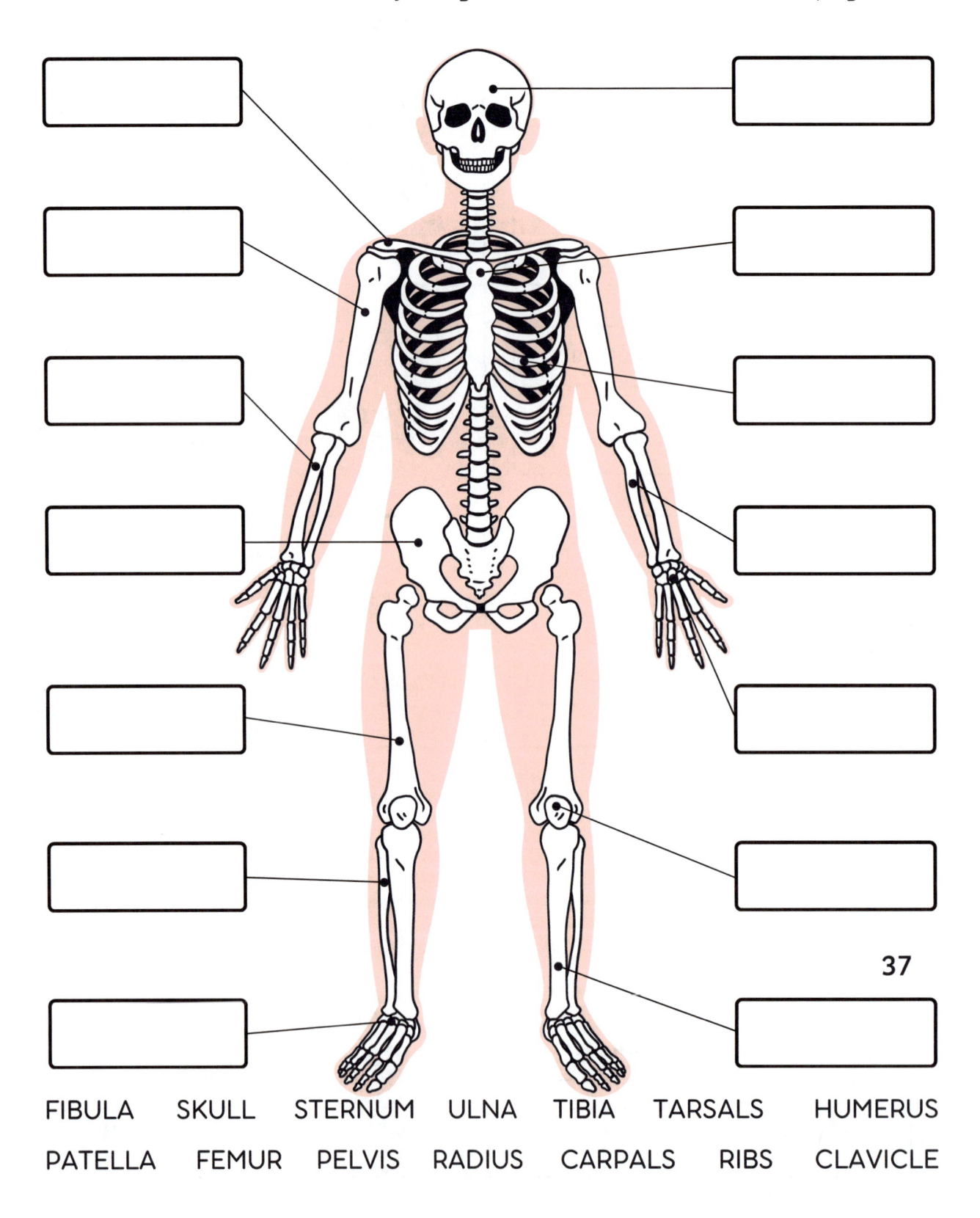

37

FIBULA   SKULL   STERNUM   ULNA   TIBIA   TARSALS   HUMERUS
PATELLA   FEMUR   PELVIS   RADIUS   CARPALS   RIBS   CLAVICLE

# Cute Skeleton

- Cut out the following skeleton pieces along their dotted lines.
- Glue all the pieces together at the junction points.

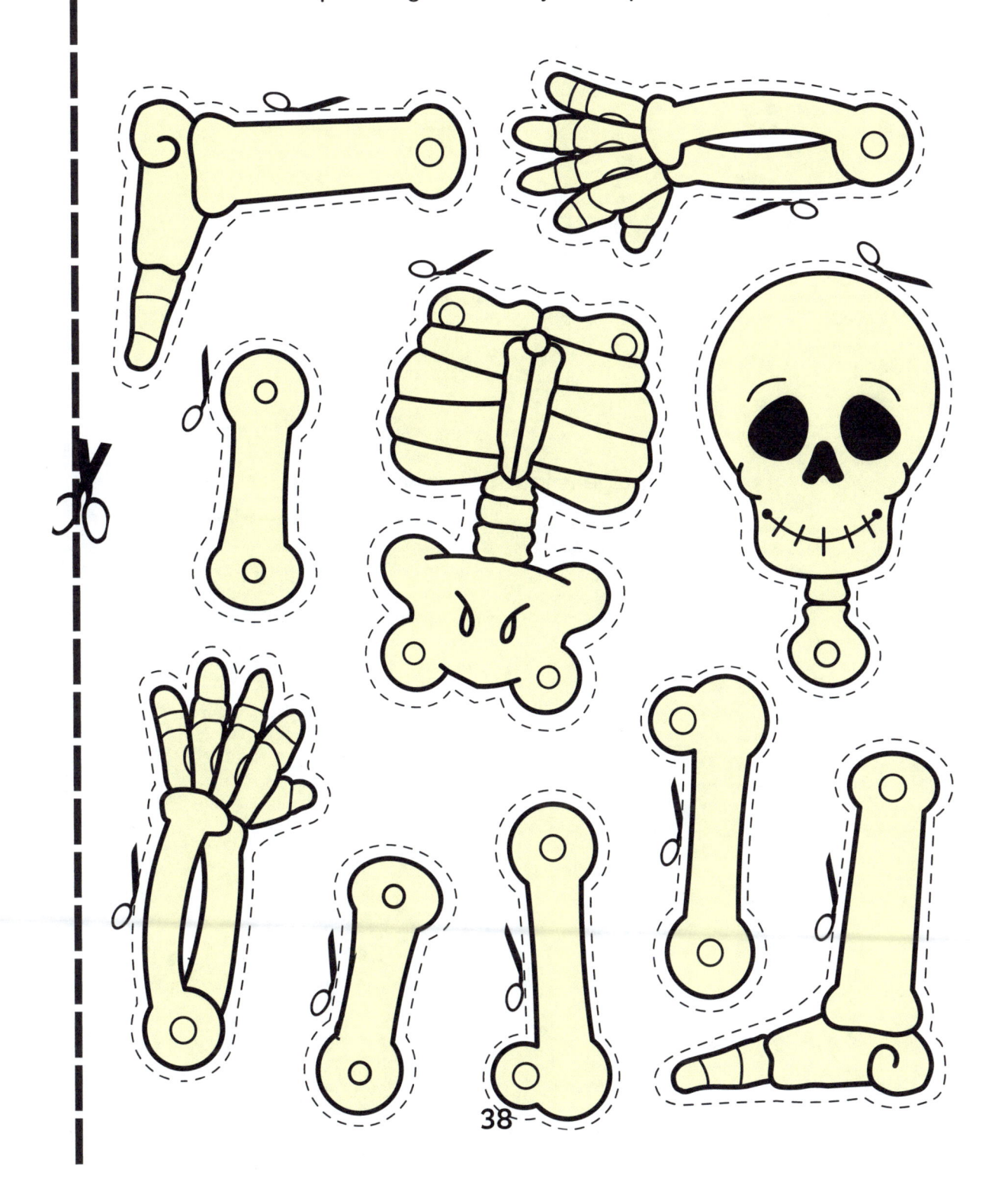

This page is intentionally left blank

This page is intentionally left blank

# Food Chain

**Direction: make arrow to connect each picture to show the food chain.**

**Mention 2 producers in the food chain above!**

**Mention 3 consumers in the food chain above!**

40

# SCIENCE HOME PROJECT

Using a Paper Plate and the information you learned about food chains create a model using a paper plate. Below is an example (use different animals)

Draft your ideas here:

Materials you will use:

1. Paper plate
2.
3.
4.
5.

Notes:

41

# Table of Content Unit 2

| Topic | Page |
|---|---|
| The Plant World | 44-45 |
| Kingdoms | 46 |
| Biodiversity | 47-53 |
| Photosynthesis | 54-62 |
| Animal Cell | 63-64 |
| Sorting Plants and Animals | 65-68 |
| Vertebrates and Invertebrates | 69-71 |
| Insects | 72-75 |
| Science Project: Butterfly Cycle | 76 |

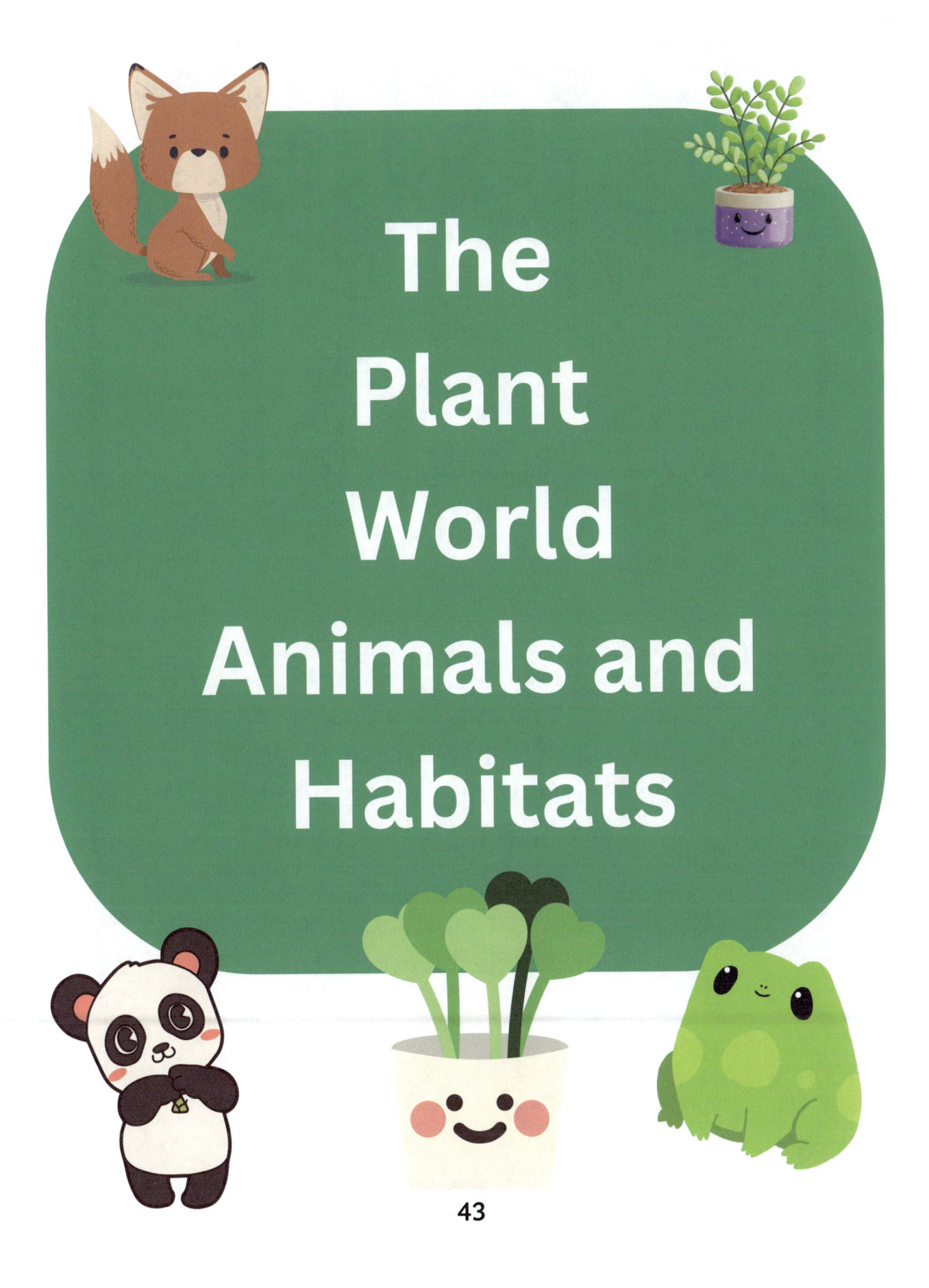

# The Plant World Animals and Habitats

# CAUTION

## WORK WITH CARE!

## SAFETY SAVES LIVES

### Safety Tips

- No horseplay will be tolerated.
- Assume that all chemicals of unknown toxicity are highly toxic.

- Avoid distracting or startling persons working in the laboratory.

# PLANT WORLD
## Find and Define New Vocabulary of this section

# Kingdom Categories

Archaea   Bacteria   Protista   Fungi   Plantae   Animalia

Look at each of the pictures below, find the Kingdom category and label it in the box next to the picture.

|  |  |
|---|---|
|  |  |
|  |  |
|  |  |
|  |  |
|  |  |
|  |  |

46

# BIODIVERSITY
## comparing habitats

What do you notice about animal and plant diversity in each of the following habitats. Use the Habitat posters to help you.

| HABITAT | PLANT OBSERVATIONS | ANIMAL OBSERVATIONS |
|---|---|---|
| TUNDRA | | |
| DESERT | | |
| AQUATIC | | |
| FOREST | | |
| GRASSLAND | | |
| WETLAND | | |

# BIOMES

A biome is a special place on Earth where plants, animals, and the weather are all alike.

Directions: Write down a living animal and plant found in the biome.

|  | Animal Life | Plant Life |
|---|---|---|
| Aquatic |  |  |
| Desert |  |  |
| Forest |  |  |
| Grassland |  |  |
| Tundra |  |  |

What biome do you live in?

What is one thing you can do to keep biomes safe?

48

# SCIENCE HOME PROJECT

Using a Shoe Box and the information you have learned about biomes to create a model of one of the biomes.

Draft your ideas here:

Materials you will use:

1. Shoe box
2.
3.
4.
5.

Notes:

# Paste Here!

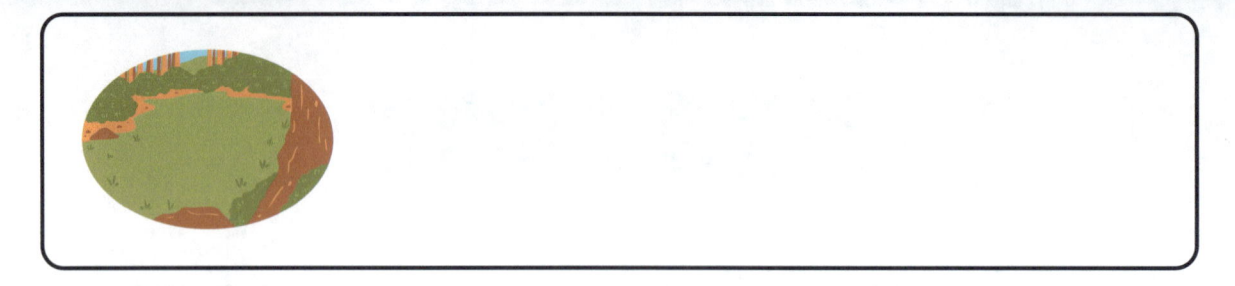

This page is intentionally left blank

# The Biomes

Cut and identify the flora and fauna at the bottom according to their biomes. Paste your cut images into the tables on the next page.

50

This page is intentionally left blank

# Biomes Around the World

Directions: Cut out the names of the biomes. Paste the words under the picture that matches that habitat.

| rainforest | desert | aquatic |

| grassland | forest | tundra |

52

This page is intentionally left blank

# ANIMALS & HABITATS

Directions: Cut out the names of the habitats. Paste the habitat label under the animal that lives in that habitat.

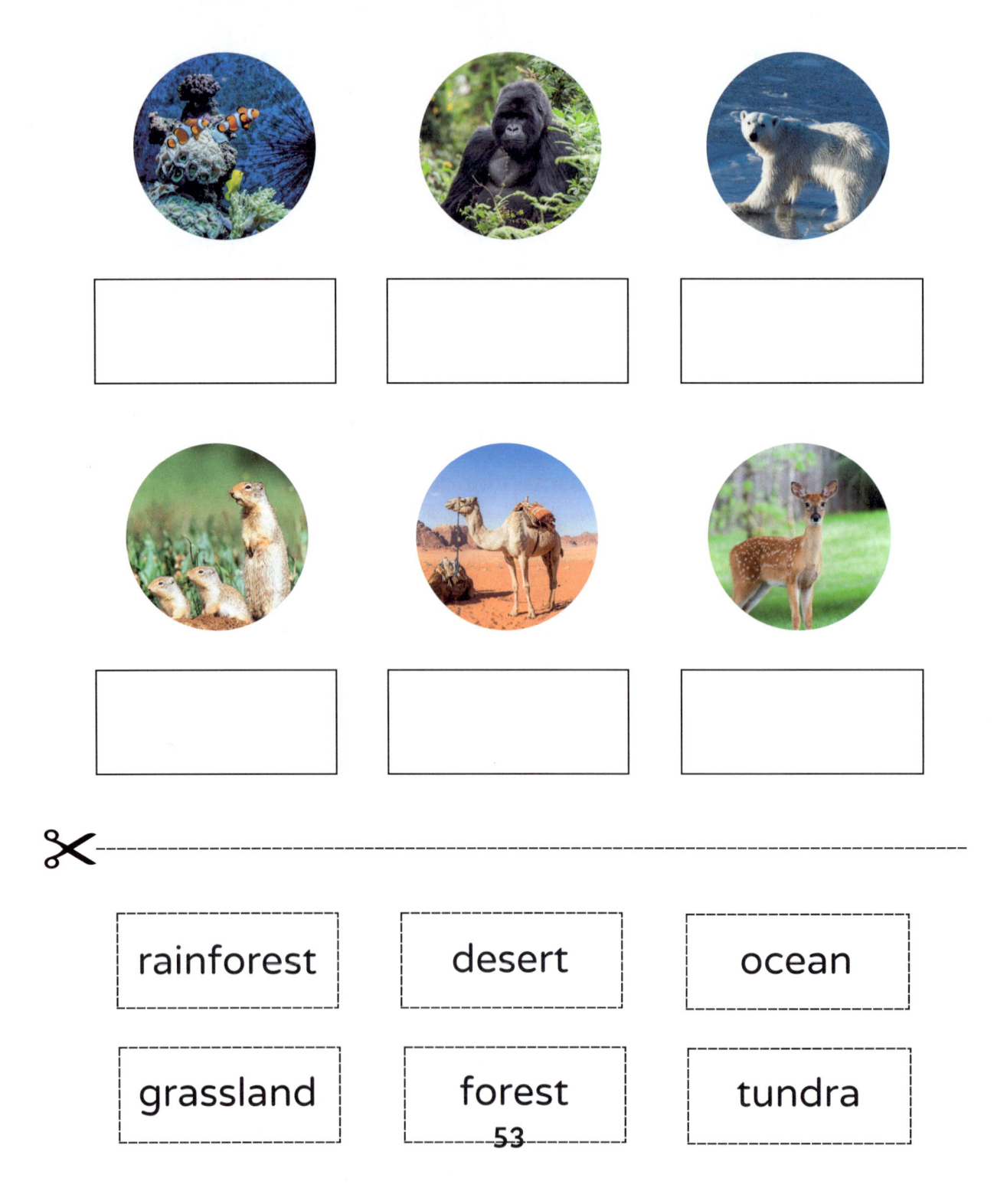

✂ -----------------------------------------------

| rainforest | desert | ocean |
| grassland | forest | tundra |

This page is intentionally left blank

# PHOTOSYNTHESIS

Task: Complete each of the questions using the diagrams provided and additional research (if necessary).

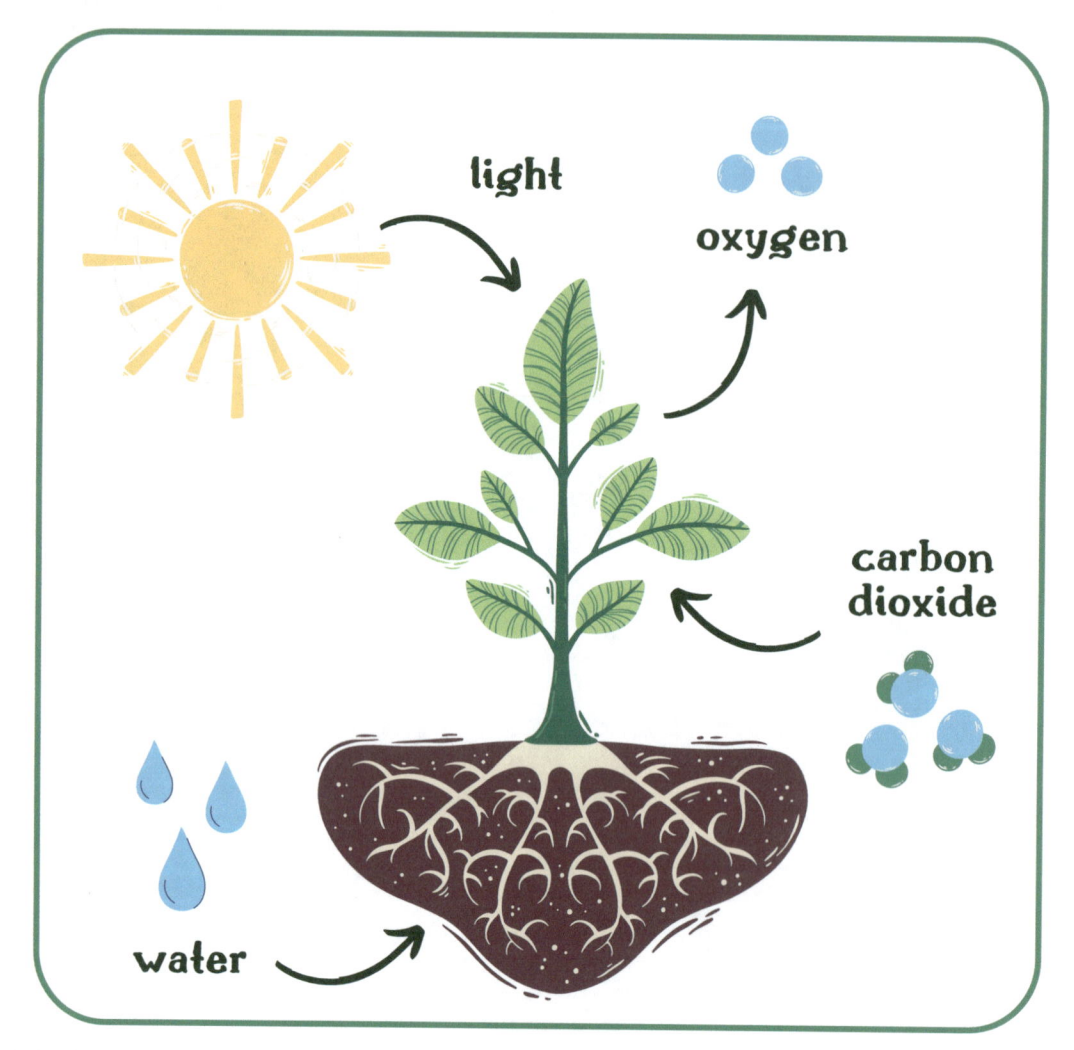

What type of organisms can photosynthesize?

_____

What is the main source of energy that drives the process of photosynthesis?

_____

**(light energy)**
**carbon dioxide + water -> glucose + oxygen**

What three 'ingredients' are required for photosynthesis to occur?
_____

Where is the water used in photosynthesis sourced from?
_____

In which cell organelle does photosynthesis take place?
_____

Where is the carbon dioxide used in photosynthesis sourced from?
_____

## CHALLENGE QUESTIONS:

What molecule absorbs sunlight during photosynthesis?
_____

How does a plant use the sugars produced through photosynthesis?
_____
_____

Why is photosynthesis important for all living organisms?
_____

Name:

Score:

Class:

Date:

# PLANT CELL

Identify and label each part of the plant cell.

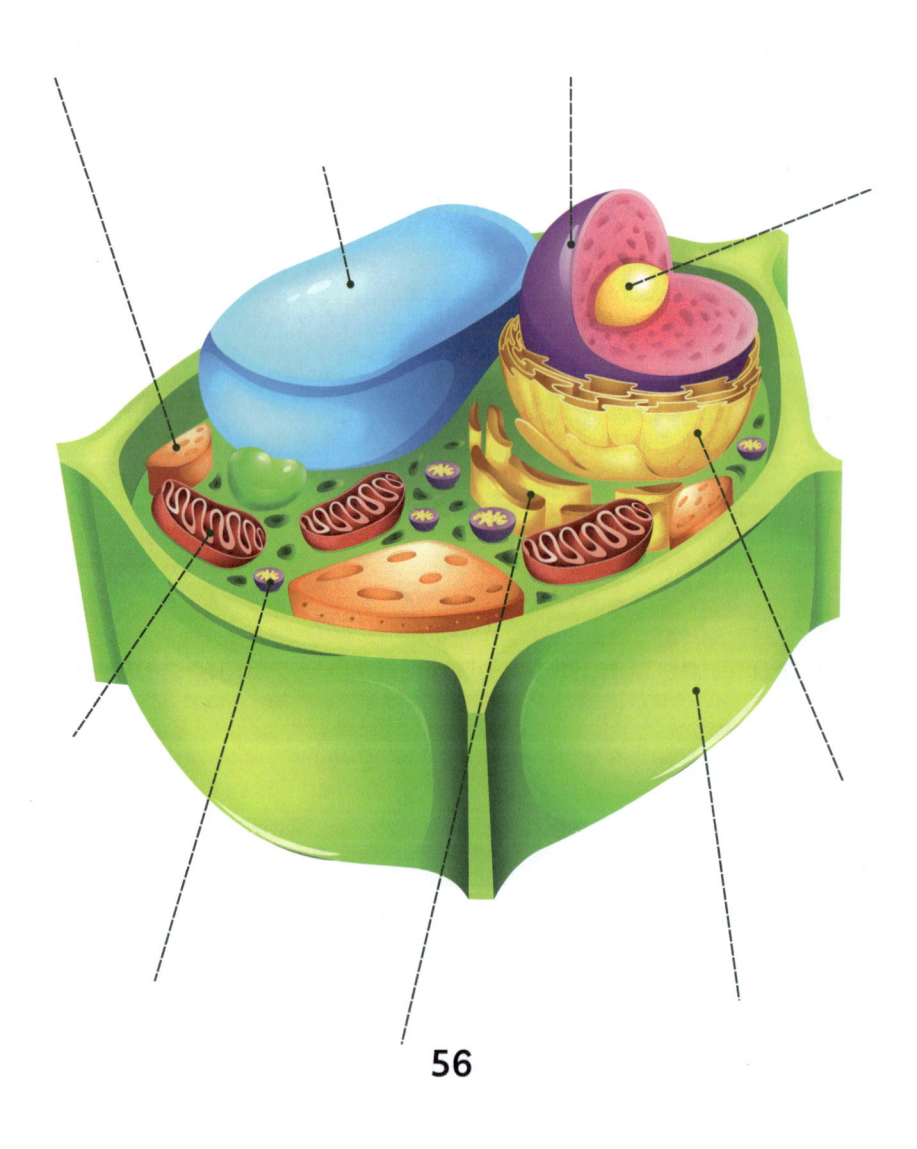

56

GRADE: _____ Out of _____

# CELLULAR STRUCTURES

Draw a line from each of the cell structures to the cell function that it matches.

- MITOCHONDRIA
- NUCLEUS
- CELL WALL
- CELL MEMBRANE
- CHLOROPLAST

- Gives the cell structure and support.
- The energy factory of the cell.
- Controls what enters and exits the cell.
- Converts light energy to chemical energy.
- Stores the DNA and controls cell activity.

# Label Me!

Direction: Label the parts of the plant.

| stem | fruit | leaf |
| roots | | flower |

58

Cut the images below. Assemble and paste them on a clean sheet of paper to illustrate the diagram of photosynthesis and cellular respiration.

Chemical Energy (ATP)

Carbon Dioxide

Photosynthesis

Oxygen

Solar Energy

Water

Cellular Respiration

Glucose

Answer key is under the resources section

This page is intentionally left blank

# PARTS OF A PLANT

Match the words on the left to its picture on the right.

flower •

seeds •

leaves •

roots •

stem •

# PLANT OBSERVATION SHEET

Based on today's observation, parts of the plant that I can see are.. (tick all boxes that apply)

| roots ☐ | leaves ☐ | stem ☐ |

| flower ☐ | fruit ☐ |

To help my plant grows, I take care of it by..
_____
_____
_____
_____

# PLANT OBSERVATION SHEET

Today is day _____ observation.

The type of seed that I plant is..
_____
_____

This is what my plant looks like:

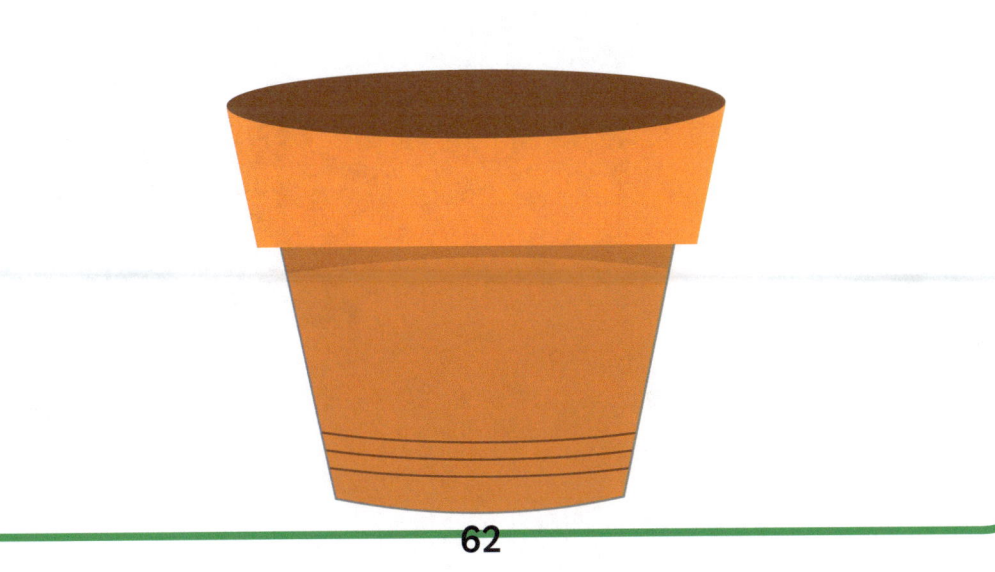

62

# TYPE OF PLANTS

Write the names of the plants on the boxes below.

tree vine flowers

herb shrubs

63

This page is intentionally left blank

# Animal Cell

Write the name of each part of the animal cell.

64

GRADE: _____ Out of _____

# THE CELL MEMBRANE

Directions: Do some online research and use the terms below to label the parts of the cell membrane.

---

Transmembrane Protein         Channel Protein

Hydrophilic Head         Hydrophobic Tail         Peripheral Protein

Integral Protein         Carbohydrate Chain

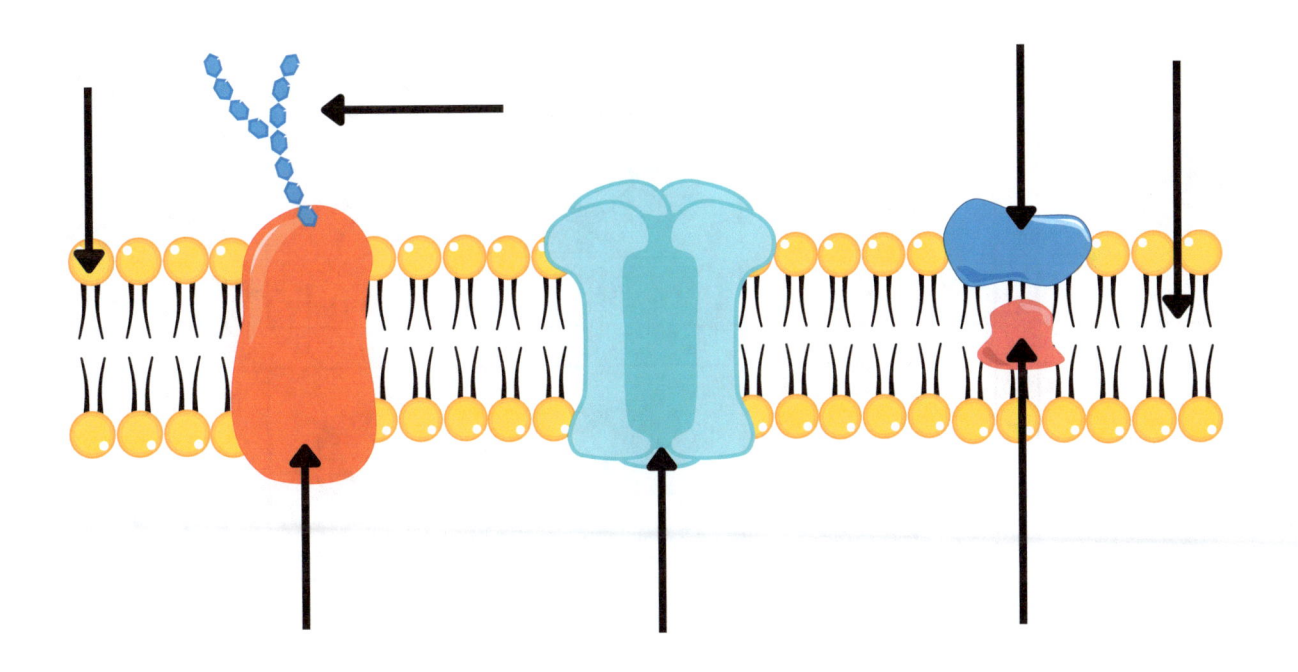

---

65

# SORTING PLANTS AND ANIMALS

Cut out pictures below and glue them into the correct box.

| PLANTS | ANIMALS |
|---|---|
|  |  |

| Elephant | Cactus | Fish | Squirrel | Shrub |
| Whale | Racoon | Pine Tree | Snail | Ivy |
| Dandelion | Ladybug | Daisy | Grass | Camel |

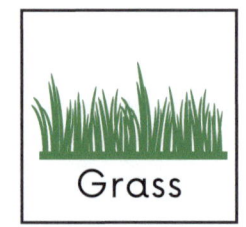

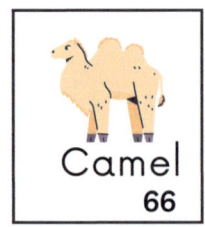

This page is intentionally left blank

# SORTING BY FARM AND FOREST

Decide if each animal below belongs in the farm or the forest, then cut out the pictures and glue them into the correct box.

## FARM

## FOREST

| donkey | duck | cow | deer | racoon |
| wolf | sheep | goose | beaver | fox |
| hedgehog | horse | owl | bison | pig |

This page is intentionally left blank

# Let's Sort

GRADE: _____ Out of _____

# SCIENCE STATIONS

Directions:
- Cut out the images below, using the dotted lines as your guide to create the sorting cards.
- Sort the cards to the correct map to indicate if the animal is vertebrate or invertebrate.

Vocabulary Words:
- Vertebrate: an animal with a backbone.
- Invertebrate: an animal without a backbone.

This page is intentionally left blank

69

This page is intentionally left blank

**VERTEBRATE**

GRADE: _____ Out of _____

This page is intentionally left blank

**INVERTEBRATE**

GRADE: _____ Out of _____

This page is intentionally left blank

GRADE: _____ Out of _____

# Body Parts of a Fish

Directions: Label the parts of the fish. Choose from the words inside the box.

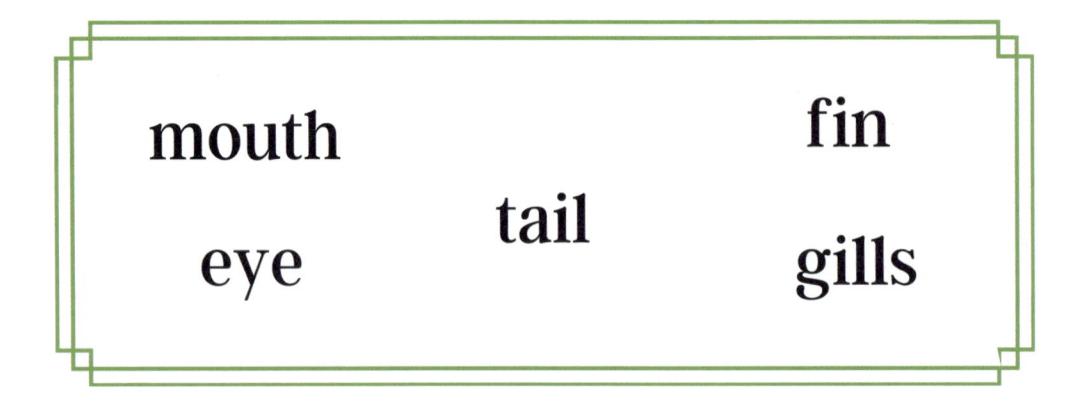

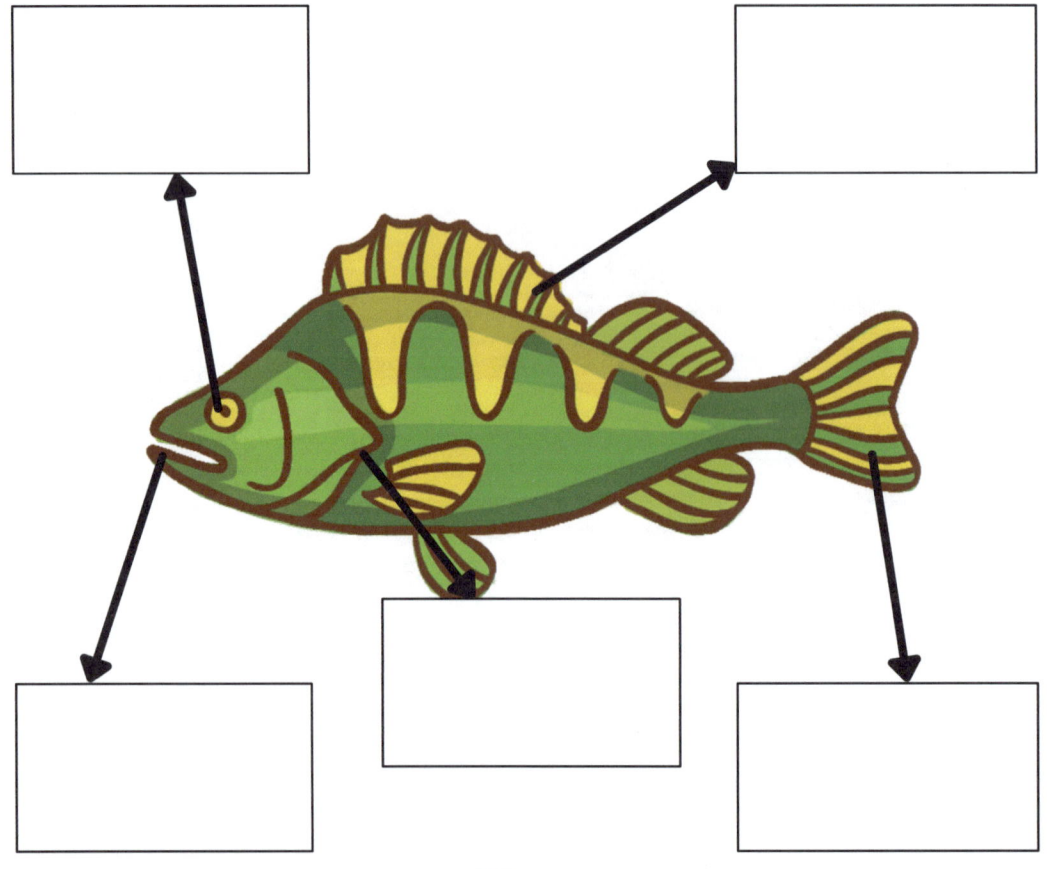

```
mouth              fin
         tail
eye                gills
```

72

# Insects

Insects are invertebrates, which means they have no backbone. Insects have six legs, antennae, and three parts to their body.

Bee

Ant

Ladybug

Cricket

Mosquito

Fly

Caterpillar

Dragonfly

Grasshopper

Praying mantis

Butterfly

# BUTTERFLY SCAVENGER HUNT

| monarch | tiger swallowtails | black swallowtail |
| --- | --- | --- |
| cabbage white | orange sulfur | spring azure |
| mourning cloak | question mark & comma | viceroy |
| gray hairstreak | wood-nymph | painted lady |

What life cycle stage?

○ egg    ○ larva    ○ pupa    ○ adult

Where did you see the monarch?

_____

_____

What is something you notice?

_____

_____

_____

monarch

What is something you wonder?

_____

_____

Write a short story about the monarch.

_____

_____

_____

_____

_____

_____

_____

# BUTTERFLY
## Life Cycle

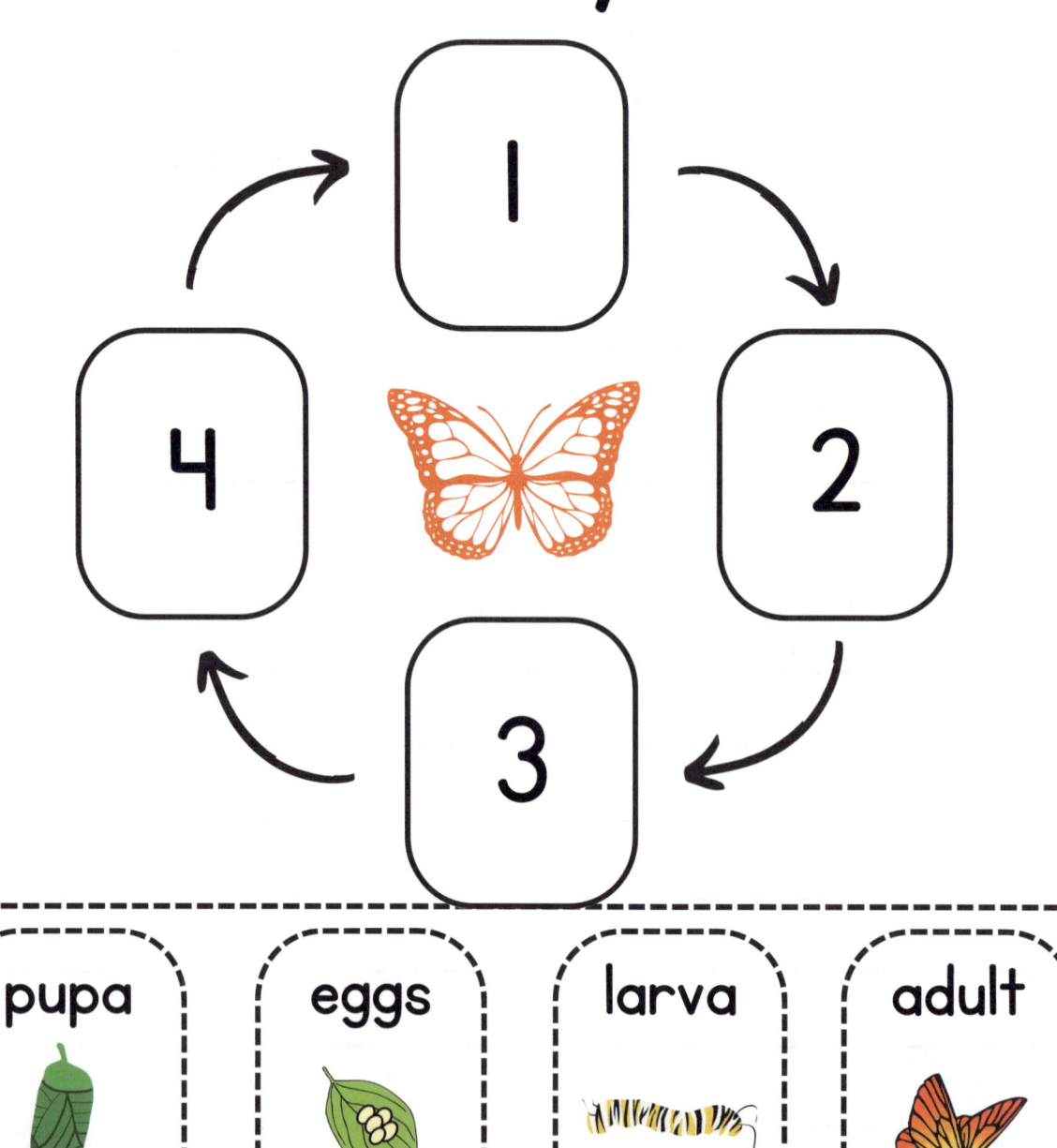

1
2
3
4

| pupa | eggs | larva | adult |

This page is intentionally left blank

# SCIENCE HOME PROJECT

Using a Paper Plate and the information you learned about the butterfly cycle to create a model using a paper plate. Below is an example.

Draft your ideas here:

Materials you will use:

1. Paper plate
2.
3.
4.
5.

Notes:

# Table of Content
# Unit 3

| Topic | Page |
|---|---|
| Scientific Method | 80-83 |
| States of Matter | 84-89 |
| Experiment: Sin is like a Thread | 90 |
| Experiment: Comparing sunflower and bean seeds | 91-95 |
| Properties of Matter | 96-97 |
| Energy Types | 98 |
|  |  |
|  |  |

# Scientific Investigation How Things Work

# CAUTION

**WORK WITH CARE!**

## SAFETY SAVES LIVES

Safety Tips:

- All containers must have appropriate labels.
- Do not taste or sniff chemicals.
- Never consume and/or store food or beverages orin areas where hazardous chemicals are used.

# Scientific Method

GRADE: _____ Out of _____

**Fill out each section of the Scientific Method as you go through your experiment!**

The purpose of this experiment is to...

I predict that...

My research tells me that...

In conclusion I found out that....

## SCIENTIFIC METHOD REPORT STEPS AND INFORMATION

GRADE: _____ Out of _____

### 1 Purpose

The purpose of the experiment is to see, or find out what?

### 2 Research

In your own words, inform the reader of what you have learnt on this topic.

### 3 Hypothesis

What is your prediction for the experiment?

### 4 Experiment

What materials did you use?
What steps did you take to put the experiment together?

### 5 Analysis and Conclusion

Analyse your data. What results do you see?

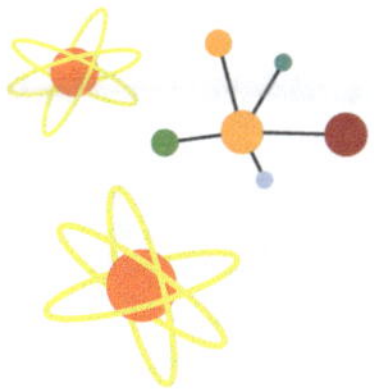

Was your hypothesis correct? Why or why not?

What would you do differently next time, if anything?

# Scientific Method

## 1. OBSERVE

Lorem ipsum dolor sit amet, consectetur adipiscing elit. Nunc fermentum urna ac dolor aliquam, vitae ultricies diam accumsan. Maecenas porttitor lectus in purus euismod, iaculis dapibus massa hendrerit. Nam vulputate ipsum vel velit sodales tincidunt.

## 2. DO SOME RESEARCH

Lorem ipsum dolor sit amet, consectetur adipiscing elit. Nunc fermentum urna ac dolor aliquam, vitae ultricies diam accumsan. Maecenas porttitor lectus in purus euismod, iaculis dapibus massa hendrerit. Nam vulputate ipsum vel velit sodales tincidunt. Fusce lacus ex, blandit ac sem eu, rutrum dignissim nisi.

## 3. FORMULATE A HYPOTHESIS

Lorem ipsum dolor sit amet, consectetur adipiscing elit. Nunc fermentum urna ac dolor aliquam, vitae ultricies diam accumsan. Maecenas porttitor lectus in purus euismod, iaculis dapibus massa hendrerit. Nam vulputate ipsum vel velit sodales tincidunt.

## 4. EXPERIMENTATION

Lorem ipsum dolor sit amet, consectetur adipiscing elit. Nunc fermentum urna ac dolor aliquam, vitae ultricies diam accumsan. Maecenas porttitor lectus in purus euismod, iaculis dapibus massa hendrerit. Nam vulputate ipsum vel velit sodales tincidunt. Fusce lacus ex, blandit ac sem eu, rutrum dignissim nisi.

## 5. ANALYZING DATA

Lorem ipsum dolor sit amet, consectetur adipiscing elit. Nunc fermentum urna ac dolor aliquam, vitae ultricies diam accumsan. Maecenas porttitor lectus in purus euismod, iaculis dapibus massa hendrerit. Nam vulputate ipsum vel velit sodales tincidunt.

## 6. COME TO A CONCLUSION

Lorem ipsum dolor sit amet, consectetur adipiscing elit. Nunc fermentum urna ac dolor aliquam, vitae ultricies diam accumsan. Maecenas porttitor lectus in purus euismod, iaculis dapibus massa hendrerit. Nam vulputate ipsum vel velit sodales tincidunt. Fusce lacus ex, blandit ac sem eu, rutrum dignissim nisi.

# PROCEDURE FOR PLANTING A SUNFLOWER

GRADE: _____ Out of _____

Using what you have learned about the scientific method plant a sunflower seed and a bean seed. Predict which will grow taller.

**Goal:**

**Materials:**

**Instructions:**

**Conclusion:**

# States of Matter

Color the picture. Cut out each state of matter below the page and paste them in their right boxes.

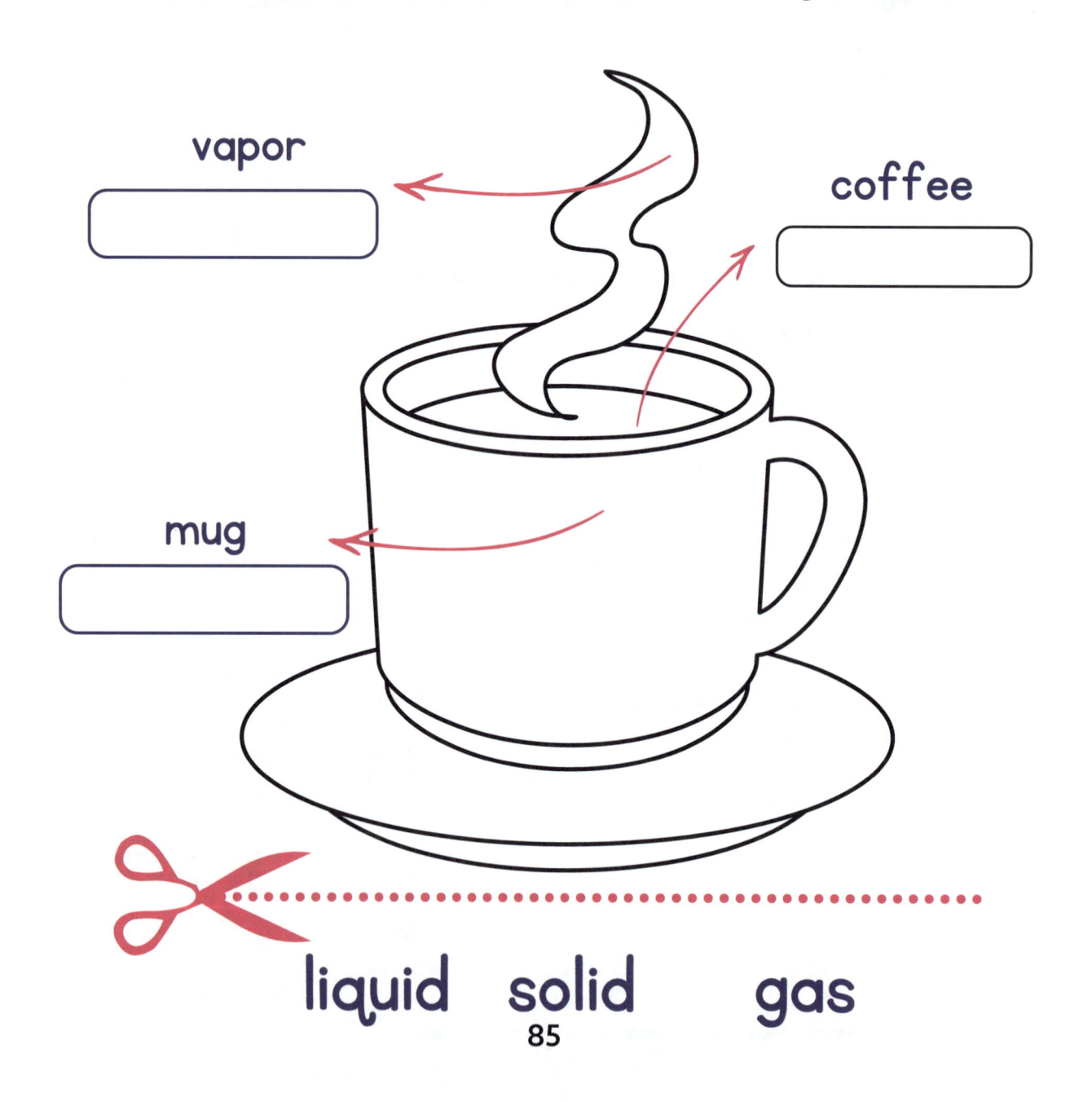

vapor

coffee

mug

liquid   solid   gas

This page is intentionally left blank

GRADE: _____ Out of _____

# GAS

Draw an example of gas

Describe the properties of gas that you draw

What is the color of the object?
------------------------------------------

What is the shape of the object?
------------------------------------------

What is the texture of the object?
------------------------------------------

Can it move on its own?
------------------------------------------

GRADE: _____ Out of _____

# SOLID

**Draw an example of solid material**

**Describe the properties of solid that you draw**

What is the color of the object?

------------------------------------------------

What is the shape of the object?

------------------------------------------------

What is the texture of the object?

------------------------------------------------

Can it move on its own?

------------------------------------------------

GRADE: _____ Out of _____

# LIQUID

Draw an example of liquid material

Describe the properties of liquid that you draw

What is the color of the object?
-----------------------------------------

What is the shape of the object?
-----------------------------------------

What is the texture of the object?
-----------------------------------------

Can it move on its own?
-----------------------------------------

GRADE: _____ Out of _____

# STATES OF MATTER

Draw examples of materials for different states of matter. Explain how each state is different.

**Solid**

_____
_____
_____
_____

**Liquid**

_____
_____
_____
_____

**Gas**

GRADE: ____ Out of ____

# States of Matter

Cut and paste the word into the correct column.

| solid | liquid | gas |
|-------|--------|-----|
|       |        |     |

- - - - - - - - - - - - - - - - - - - - - - - - - - - - - -

wind | shoe | smoke | juice

soda | wood | book | apple

river | rain | soap | air

This page is intentionally left blank

**GRADE: \_\_\_\_ Out of \_\_\_\_\_**

Fill in the graphic organizer about matter.

| Characteristics of Particles of Matter | Examples of Solid |
|---|---|
| Examples of Liquid | Examples of Gas |

**Matter**

# Sin is Like a Thread

God is the creator of the World. He sent Jesus so we could be saved. To be saved we must accept Jesus as our Savior. To live for Jesus, we should obey God's commandments.To disobey God is a sin.

Sin is like a thread. Once a person decides to disobey God they get tangled in sin. The more we sin, the harder it becomes to stay away from sin. The thread becomes stronger and only Jesus can get us out.

## Materials

1-sewing thread (preferably black)
2-ruler
3-scissors

## Directions

Give each child a long piece of thread, a ruler and scissor. Ask students to measure 12 inches of thread and to cut and discard the extra thread. Now choose a person (preferably another adult). The person chosen must place their hands together (as if praying). Ask two students to tie their threads tight on the adult hands. Now tell the kids sin is like those threads and ask the adult to break them off (it should be easy to break).

Now repeat the process by asking all students to come up and tie their threads around the hands of the adult. After all the children are done explain that a person who is sinning hets tied up like that. Then ask the adult to try to break the threads off ( it should be impossible). Now explain that sin may look "ok" for a while but that it will tangle the person and only Jesus can save us.

GRADE: _____ Out of _____

# CHANGES IN MATTER

**Identify whether a given situation is a physical or chemical change. Write PC for physical change and CC for chemical change.**

1. A piece of paper is torn in half.
2. A banana turns brown after being left out for a few days.
3. Ice cubes are left out on a warm day and melt into liquid.
4. A nail rusts after being exposed to air and moisture.
5. A piece of bread is toasted in a toaster and turns brown.
6. A glass of water is heated and starts to boil.
7. Mixing vinegar and baking soda, causing a fizzy reaction.
8. Carving a piece of wood into a bird sculpture.

**Label whether a given illustration is a physical or chemical change. Write PC for physical change and CC for chemical change.**

GRADE: _____ Out of _____

# CHANGES IN STATES OF MATTER

Complete the drawings below to represent changes in states of matter.

**Melting**

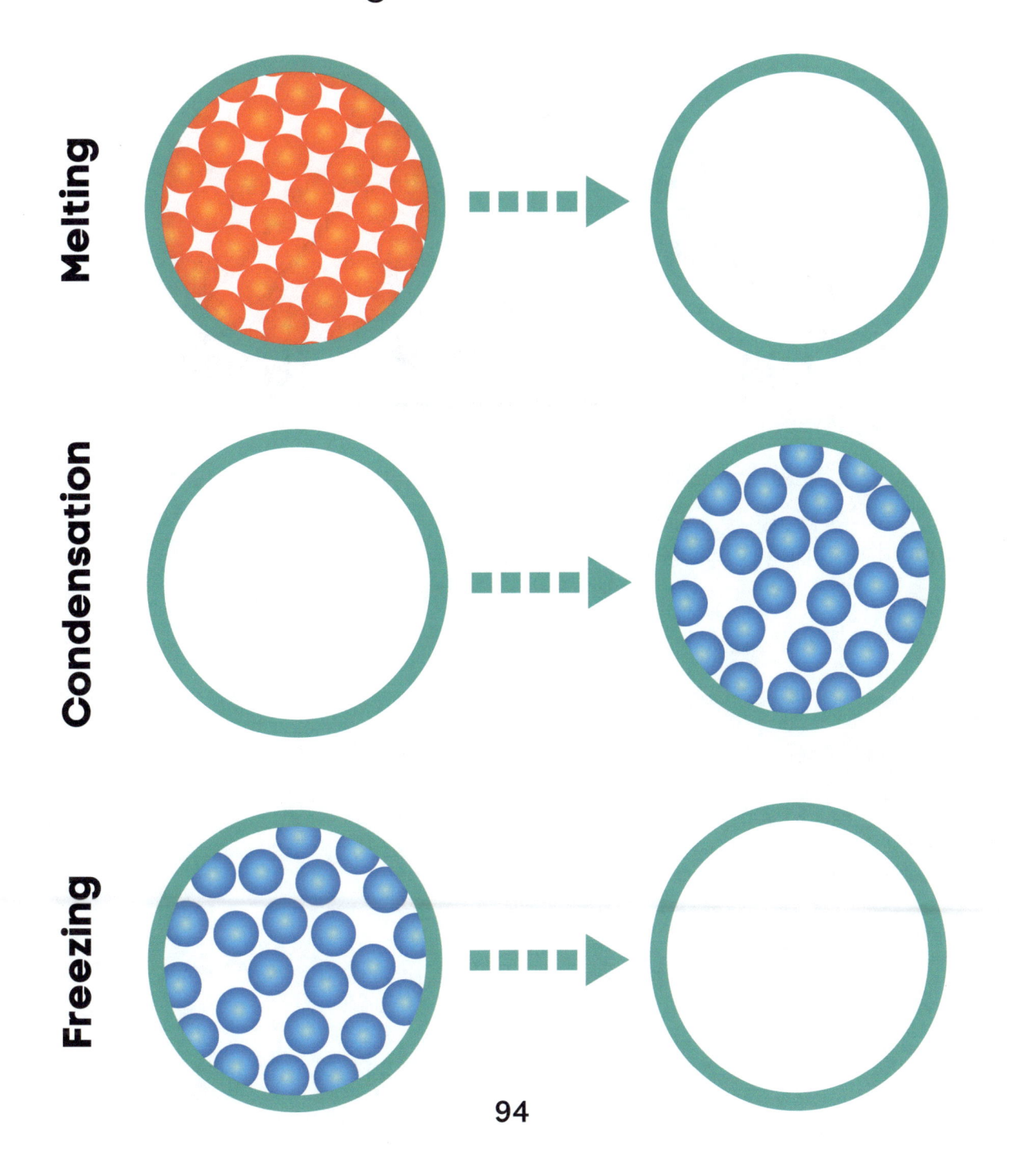

**Condensation**

**Freezing**

GRADE: _____ Out of _____

# CHANGE OF STATE

Use the diagram below to answer the following question about change of state!

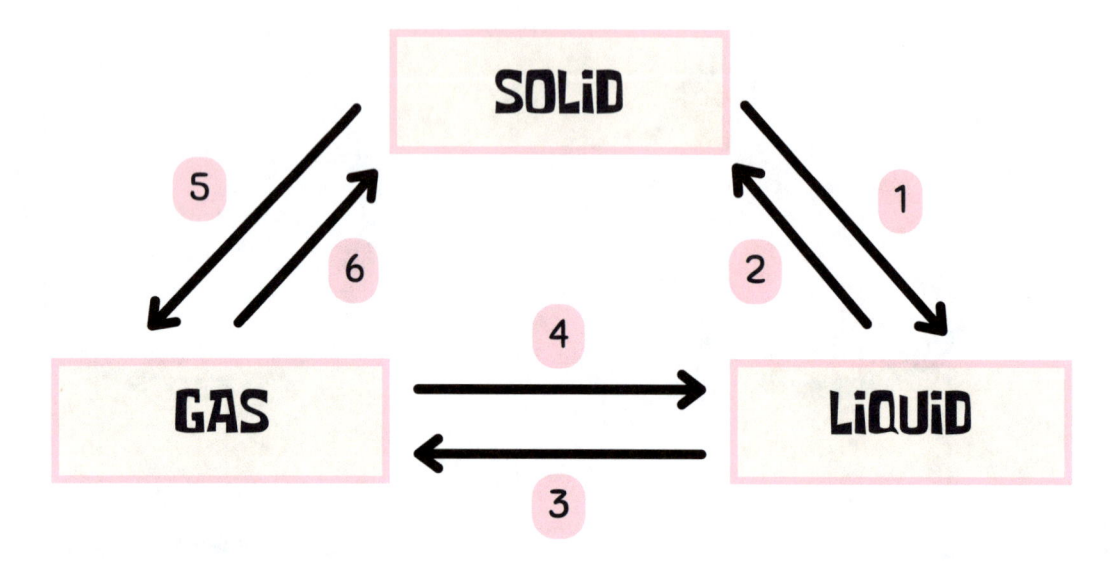

```
            SOLID
        ↙↗        ↖↘
       5  6      1  2
    ↙              ↘
   GAS  ←——3——  LIQUID
        ——4——→
```

Name the change of state of matter from:

| | |
|---|---|
| 1. Solid to liquid | 1 |
| 2. Liquid to solid | 2 |
| 3. Liquid to Gas | 3 |
| 4. Gas to liquid | 4 |
| 5. Solid to gas | 5 |
| 6. Gas to solid | 6 |

# PROPERTIES OF MATERIALS

**GRADE: _____ Out of _____**

Draw or list materials that have the following properties:

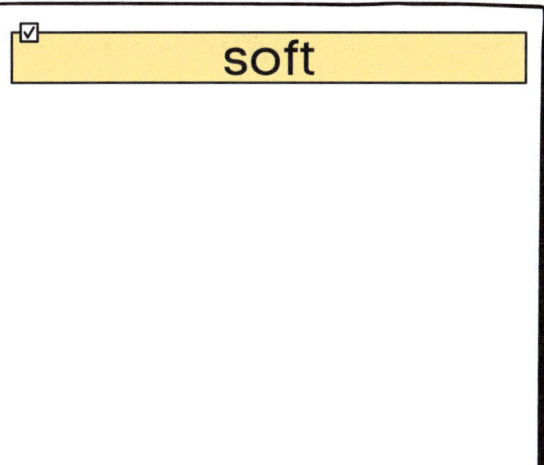

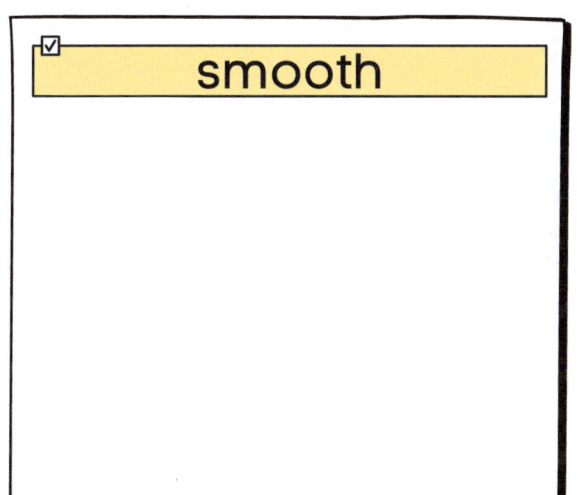

| ☑ hard | ☑ soft |
| --- | --- |
| ☑ rough | ☑ smooth |
| ☑ flexible | ☑ fluffy |

GRADE: _____ Out of _____

# Glass, Metal or Wood?

Cut out the pictures below and paste into the correct column.

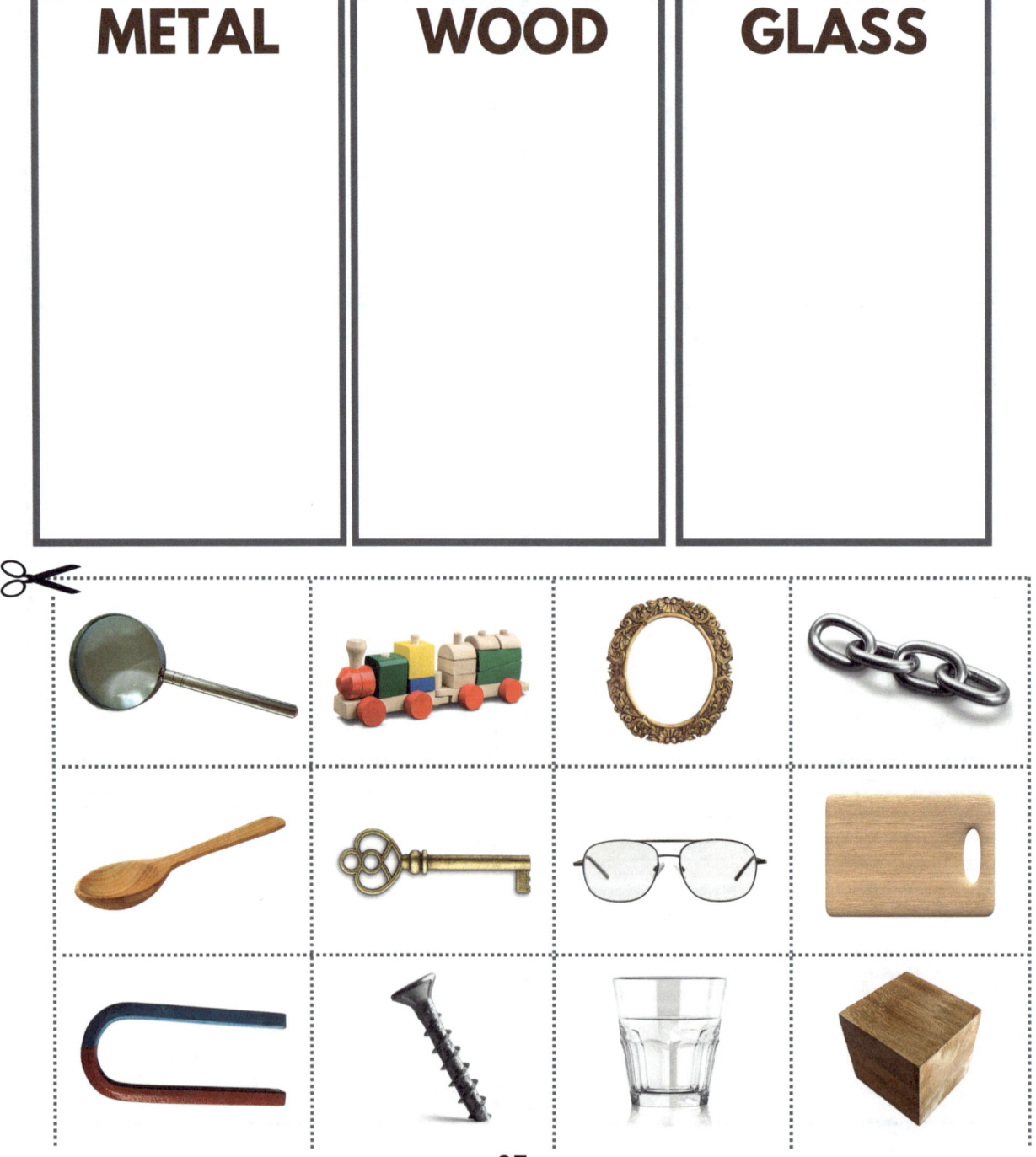

| METAL | WOOD | GLASS |
|---|---|---|
|  |  |  |

97

This page is intentionally left blank

# MATTER
## SEARCH A WORD

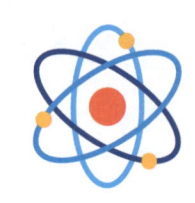

| M | A | T | T | E | R | T |
|---|---|---|---|---|---|---|
| L | S | O | L | I | D | G |
| I | S | P | A | C | E | A |
| Q | Y | R | E | A | S | S |
| U | G | A | T | O | M | D |
| I | V | O | L | U | M | E |
| D | I | M | A | S | S | T |

**Search for all the words in the list bellow:**

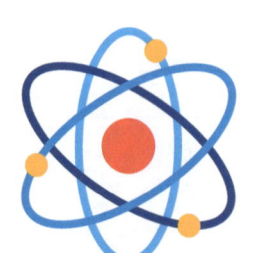

- matter
- solid
- liquid
- gas
- atom
- volume
- mass
- space

**GRADE: ____ Out of ____**

# ENERGY TYPES

Tick clean energy types and cross dirty energy types.

99

# Table of Content Unit 4

| Topic | Page |
|---|---|
| Bodies of Water | 104 |
| Continents and Oceans | 106-107 |
| Water Cycle | 108 |
| Experiment: Sink or Float predictions | 109 |
| Layers of the Earth' Atmosphere | 110 |
| Project: Solar System Model | 111-121 |
| Recycling is Everyone's Responsibility | 122-123 |
| Natural Disasters | 124-127 |
| Save the Earth | 128-135 |
| Teacher Resources & Answer Keys | 136 |

# CAUTION

**WORK WITH CARE!**

## SAFETY SAVES LIVES

Safety Tips:

- Goggles should be worn in any area where chemicals are used.

- Closed-toe shoes must be worn at all times in the laboratory. Perforated shoes or sandals are not appropriate.

# The Air Around Us
# Earth and Space

# THE ATMOSPHERE
## Find and Define New Vocabulary of this section

# BODIES OF WATER

Write the name of the following bodies of water on the box.

Ocean    Pond    River

Lake    Stream

104

# Bodies of Water

Label the diagram of Earth's water forms using the keywords below.

| Sea | River |
|---|---|
| Waterfalls | Lake |
| Pond ||

105

# Continents And Oceans

Look at the pictures and write the names of the continents and oceans

| Africa | Atlantic Ocean | Pacific Ocean | Antarctica |
| Asia | Arctic Ocean | Indian Ocean | Oceania |
| Europe | South America | North America | Continents |

# my notes

date

# WATER CYCLE

Draw the water cycle diagram. Use the word bank below.

## WORD BANK

condensation          precipitation

evaporation           accumulation

GRADE: _____ Out of _____

# Sink or Float Predictions

**Make a prediction in the table below if you think the item will float or sink.**

| Object | Float | Sink |
|---|---|---|
| pencil | | |
| paper clip | | |
| notecard | | |
| marshmallow | | |
| toy car | | |
| coin | | |
| stick | | |
| crayon | | |

# LAYERS OF THE EARTH'S ATMOSPHERE

Write two distinct facts describing each layer of the atmosphere.

Exosphere
1.
2.

Thermosphere
1.
2.

Mesosphere
1.
2.

Stratosphere
1.
2.

Troposphere
1.
2.

# SCIENCE HOME PROJECT

Using a Shoe Box and the information on the next page create a model of the solar system

Draft your ideas here:

Materials you will use:

1. Shoe Box
2.
3.
4.
5.

Notes:

# THE SOLAR SYSTEM

1. Sun
2. Mercury
3. Venus
4. Earth
5. Mars
6. Jupiter
7. Saturn
8. Uranus
9. Neptune

Mercury

Venus

Earth

Neptune

Sun

Mars

Uranus

Saturn

Jupiter

# JUPITER

Jupiter is the fifth planet from the sun. It is the largest planet in the solar system. Jupiter is a gas giant planet composed of hydrogen and helium. It is bigger than all other planets combined. Jupiter has 79 moons.

# VENUS

Venus is the second planet from the sun and is 67 million miles away from it. Venus is the Closest planet to Earth. Venus' atmosphere is composed of carbon dioxide and clouds of sulfuric acid. It is the hottest planet, reaching temperatures of 864°F. Venus has no moons.

# MERCURY

Mercury is the smallest planet in the solar system. It is the closest planet to the sun and it has a solid surface. Mercury is a heavily cratered surface with many cliffs and valleys. It is one of the coldest planets and it has no moons.

# EARTH

Earth is the third planet from the sun and is 93 million miles away from it. It is a terrestrial planet that is able to sustain life. Earth has a diverse range of environments including land masses, oceans and atmosphere.

Members of a community live together and have responsibilities in their community.

Planet Earth

# NEPTUNE

Neptune is the eighth and farthest planet from the sun. It is 2.8 billion miles away from the sun. Neptune is the third largest planet in the Solar System. Neptune is a gas giant planet composed of hydrogen, helium and methane. It has a small rocky core.

# MARS

Mars is the fourth planet from the sun. It is the second closest planet to Earth and the fourth smallest planet in Solar System. Mars is half the size of earth and has two moons. It is called the 'red planet' due to rust on its surface. Mars has largest volcano and deepest canyon.

# URANUS

Uranus is the seventh planet from the sun. it is the third largest planet in the solar system. Uranus is a gas giant composed of hydrogen, helium and methane. The methane gives it its distinctive blue-green color. Uranus has 27 moons.

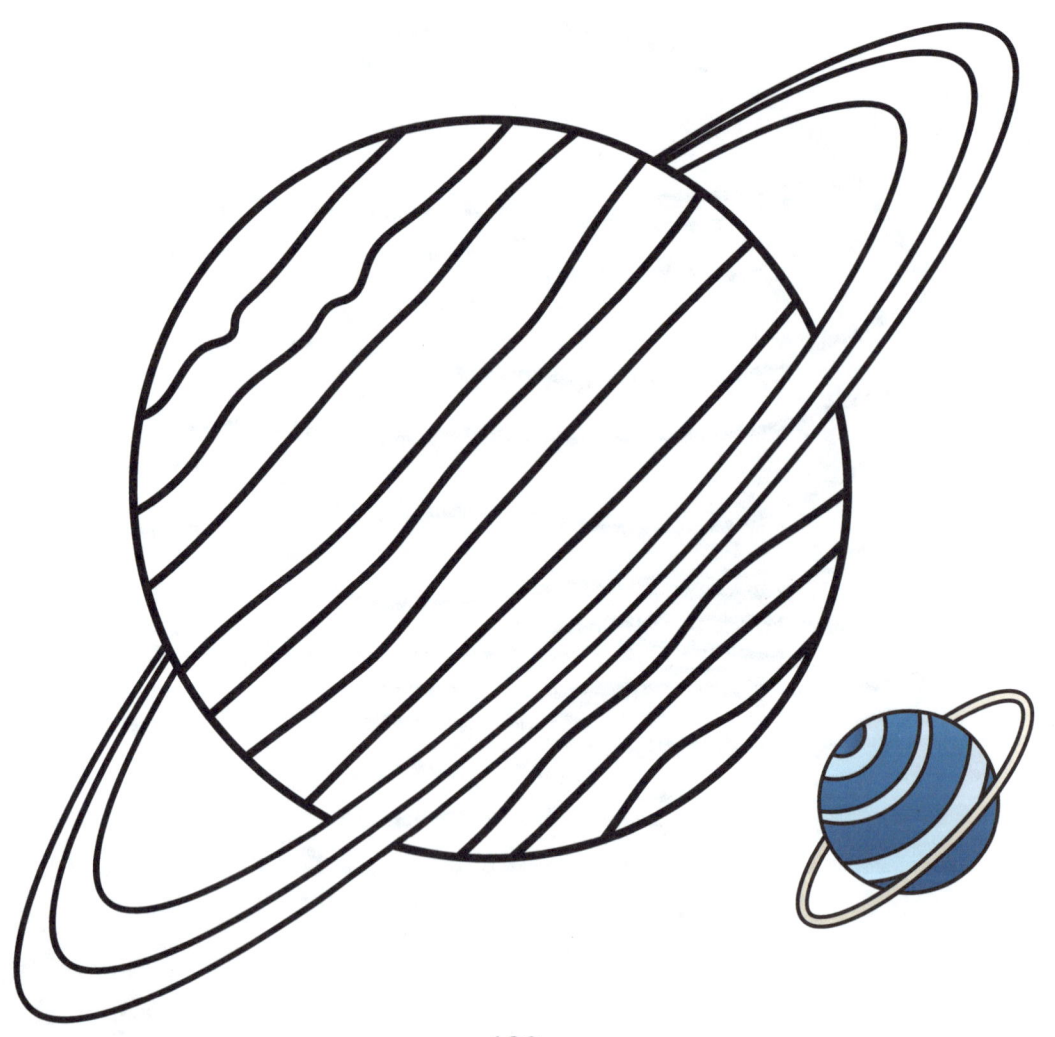

# SATURN

Saturn is the sixth planet from the sun. It is the second largest planet in the Solar System. Saturn is a gas giant and is composed of hydrogen and helium. It has a small rocky core. Saturn has 82 moons!

# Recycling is Everyone's Responsibility

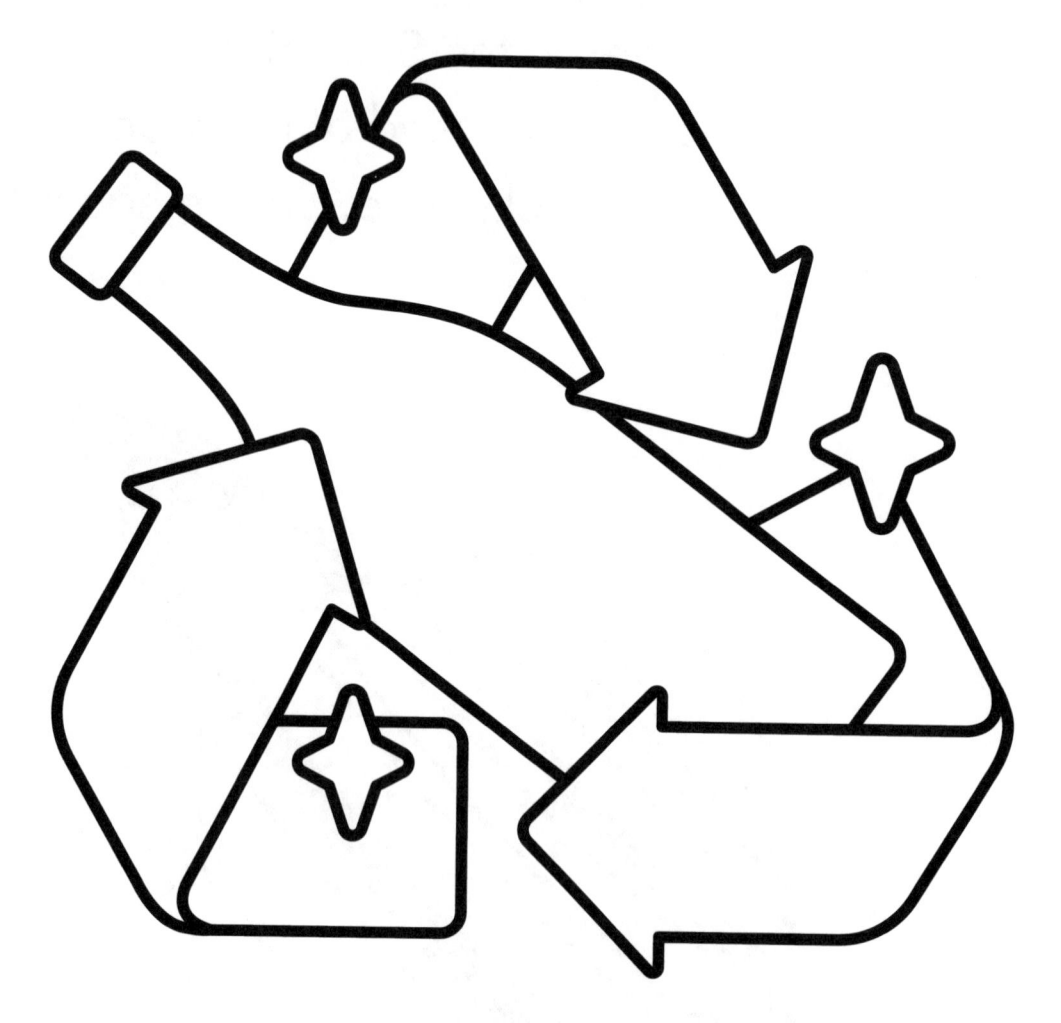

Recycle, Reduce, Reuse

In all the work you are doing, work the best you can.
Work as if you were working for the Lord, not for men...
-Colossians 3:23

GRADE: _____ Out of _____

# Love your Planet

Put a (♡) on the box if the pictures show care and concern for our planet Earth.

GRADE: _____ Out of _____

# NATURAL DISASTERS

## A- Number the pictures.

1-avalanche   2-earthquake   3-flood   4-drought   5-tornado
6-tsunami   7-forest fire   8-hurricane   9-volcano   10-landslide

124

GRADE: _____ Out of _____

# NATURAL DISASTERS

A. Match the pictures to the names of the natural disasters. Write the number inside the circle.

| 1 drought | 4 flash flood | 7 wildfire |
| 2 volcanic eruption | 5 avalanche | 8 landslide |
| 3 tornado | 6 earthquake | 9 thunderstorm |

**GRADE: ____ Out of _____**

## B-Read and name the natural disasters.

1. A mass of snow, ice and rock that slide rapidly down the side of a mountain: _____

2. a sudden violent movement of the earth's surface, sometimes causing great damage: _____

3. a large amount of water covering an area that is usually dry: _____

4. a long period when there is little or no rain: _____

5. a dangerous storm which is a spinning cone of wind that destroys anything in its path: _____

6. a mass of rock and earth moving suddenly and quickly down a steep slope: _____

7. a strong tropical storm with high winds and heavy rain: _____

8. a mountain made from burned materials that may throw out hot rocks and lava: _____

9. a fire burning in an area of land with many trees, that is difficult to control and sometimes spreads quickly: _____

10. a very large and dangerous ocean wave that is caused by an earthquake under the sea: _____

B. Write the name of the natural disaster described below.

|  |  |
|--|--|
| ☐ | It is the result when the Earth's tectonic plates suddenly shifts and the ground violently shakes. |
| ☐ | It refers to any substantial flow of rock or debris down a slope. |
| ☐ | Both earthquakes and underwater volcanic eruptions, which can result in seismic waves propagating across the ocean, are the usual causes of these waves. |
| ☐ | a prolonged period of time during which drier-than-normal circumstances cause a shortage of water. |
| ☐ | a prolonged period of time during which drier-than-normal circumstances cause a shortage of water. |

C. Draw the natural disaster inside the box and describe its cause and effect.

**NATURAL DISASTER:** _____

**CAUSE**
_____
_____
_____

**EFFECT**
_____
_____
_____

127

# Earth Day

GRADE: _____ Out of _____

Look at the pictures and circle the correct words

| | | | |
|---|---|---|---|
| 🌍 | Earth / Mars | ♻️ | Revitalize / Recycle |
| ⛰️ | Plants / Mountains | ↺ | Reuse / Conserve |
| 💧 | Land / Water | ☀️🔋 | Solar Panel / Garden |
| 🌱 | Plant / Air | 🏷️ | Recyclable cup / Recycle tag |
| 🌲 | Field / Forest | 🛍️ | Plastic bag / Reusable bag |

128

# Earth Day

Look at the pictures and circle the correct words

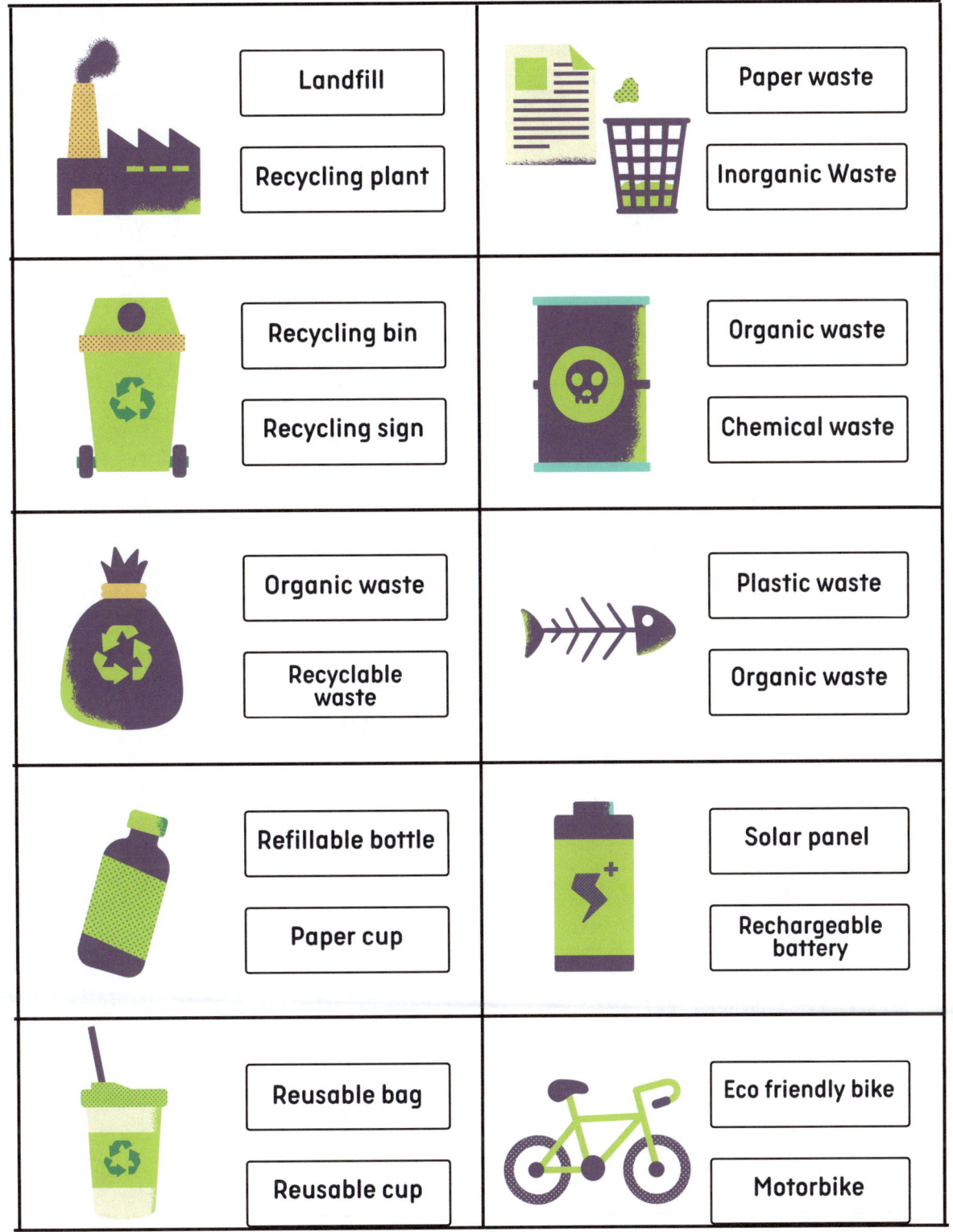

| | | | |
|---|---|---|---|
| | Landfill / Recycling plant | | Paper waste / Inorganic Waste |
| | Recycling bin / Recycling sign | | Organic waste / Chemical waste |
| | Organic waste / Recyclable waste | | Plastic waste / Organic waste |
| | Refillable bottle / Paper cup | | Solar panel / Rechargeable battery |
| | Reusable bag / Reusable cup | | Eco friendly bike / Motorbike |

# SAVE THE EARTH

We only have one Earth and we must protect it.
However, there are some negative effects of human activities on Earth.
Fill in the tables below to raise awareness about environmental issues.

| **FOREST FIRES** | **CUTTING DOWN TREES** |
|---|---|
| REASONS: | REASONS: |
| RESULTS: | RESULTS: |
| HOW TO PREVENT: | HOW TO PREVENT: |

# SAVE THE EARTH

We only have one Earth and we must protect it.
However, there are some negative effects of human activities on Earth.
Look at the example and fill in the tables below to raise awareness.

| AIR POLLUTION | WATER POLLUTION |
|---|---|
| REASONS: | REASONS: |
| RESULTS: | RESULTS: |
| HOW TO PREVENT: | HOW TO PREVENT: |

# SAVE THE EARTH

We only have one Earth and we must protect it.
However, there are some negative effects of human activities on Earth.
Look at the example and fill in the tables below to raise awareness.

| GREENHOUSE EFFECT | HUNTING ANIMALS |
|---|---|
| REASONS: | REASONS: |
| RESULTS: | RESULTS: |
| HOW TO PREVENT: | HOW TO PREVENT: |

# SAVE THE EARTH

We only have one Earth and we must protect it.
However, there are some negative effects of human activities on Earth.
Look at the example and fill in the tables below to raise awareness.

**WASTE DISPOSAL**

REASONS:

RESULTS:

HOW TO PREVENT:

**CONTAMINATION**

REASONS:

RESULTS:

HOW TO PREVENT:

# SYSTEMS OF MEASUREMENT

Directions: Use the terms below to label the missing pieces of the flow chart.

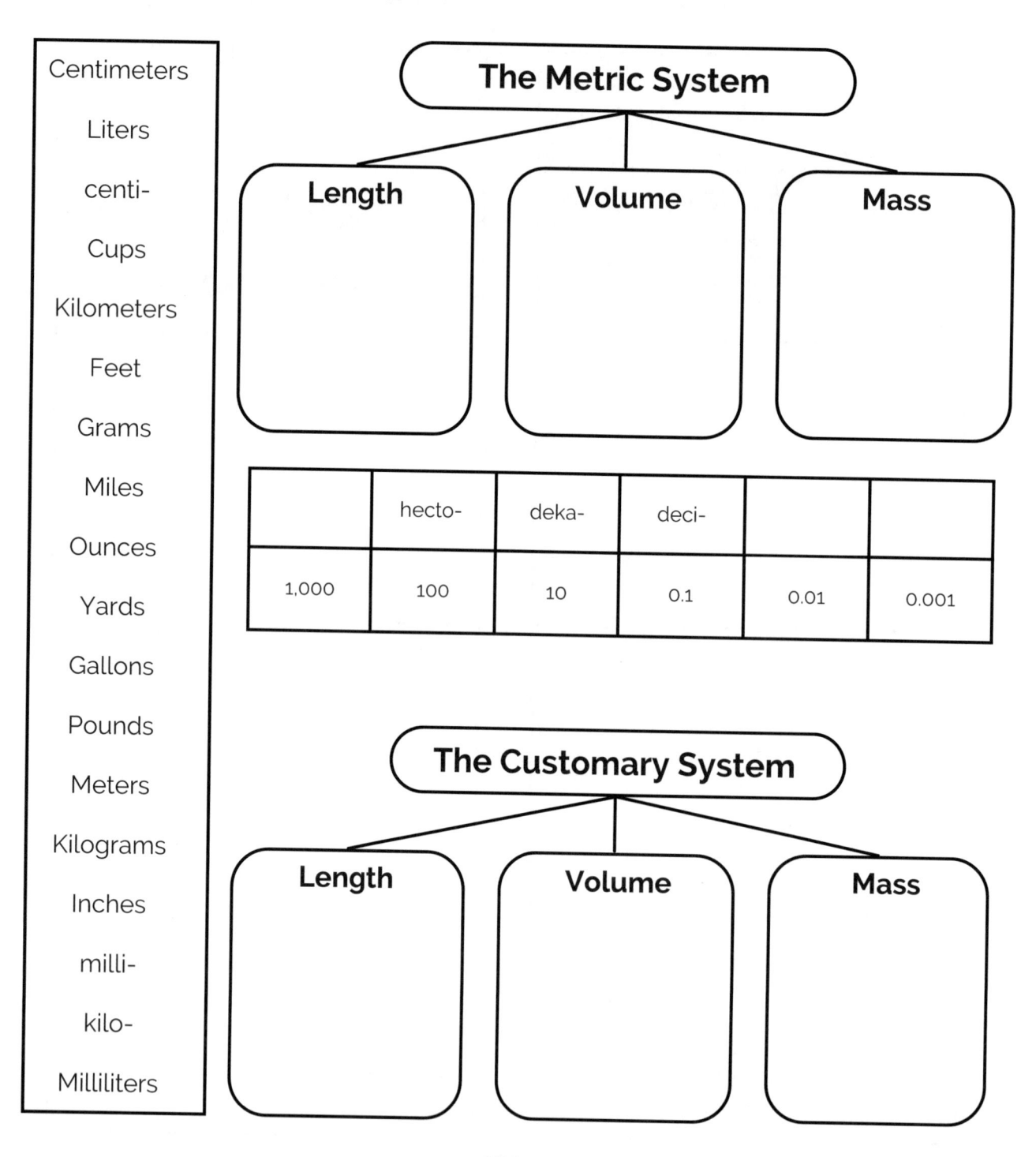

Centimeters
Liters
centi-
Cups
Kilometers
Feet
Grams
Miles
Ounces
Yards
Gallons
Pounds
Meters
Kilograms
Inches
milli-
kilo-
Milliliters

**The Metric System**
- Length
- Volume
- Mass

|  | hecto- | deka- |  | deci- |  |  |
|---|---|---|---|---|---|---|
| 1,000 | 100 | 10 | 0.1 | 0.01 | 0.001 |

**The Customary System**
- Length
- Volume
- Mass

# Simple Machines

Decide which simple machine is shown in each picture and write the name of the machine on the blank provided.

1. _____

2. _____

3. _____

4. _____

5. _____

6. _____

7. _____

8. _____

9. _____

10. _____

135

# Resources Section

# Jesus Can Save my Community

## Who is Jesus?

Adam and Eve were created by God; he gave them instructions to take care of the garden of Eden. God also told them to not eat from the tree of knowledge. They listen to the snake who was used by the devil to trick them; and disobeyed God.

God sent his only son Jesus Christ to Earth to save us. Jesus died on a cross for our sins. Anyone who believes Jesus is the son of God and accepts him as the savior will be forgiven.

Color the cross

# SCIENCE ACTIVITY

------------------------------------------------------------

Title of the Experiment

Prediction: What do you think will happen?

Draw your prediction here

*How are the three eggs like people?*

# SCIENCE QUIZ TRACKER

| Date | Grade | Notes |
|------|-------|-------|
|      |       |       |
|      |       |       |
|      |       |       |
|      |       |       |
|      |       |       |
|      |       |       |
|      |       |       |
|      |       |       |
|      |       |       |
|      |       |       |

# FIELD TRIP REFLECTION

WHAT WAS YOUR FAVORITE PART OF OUR FIELD TRIP?

_____
_____
_____

DRAW THE MOST INTERESTING THING YOU SAW TODAY.

RATE OUR FIELD TRIP AND WRITE A REVIEW.

☆ ☆ ☆ ☆ ☆

_____
_____
_____

# T Chart
**Graphic Organizer**

Organise your information using the headings below.

Topic:

| Similarities | Differences |
|---|---|
|  |  |

# STEM LAB SHEET

## ASK
What is your challenge?

## IMAGINE
What are your ideas for the challenge?

## PLAN
Draw your design.

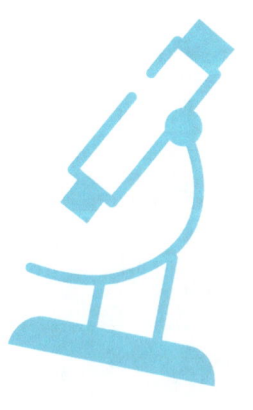

# STEM LAB SHEET

## CREATE
The finished design looks like;

## TEST
Was your plan successful?

## IMPROVE
What changes you made in your design to improve it.

## REFLECT
What did you learn from the activity?
What worked? What did not work?

Graph:

# My Research

Fact: _____
Evidence: _____
_____
_____
Source: _____

Fact: _____
Evidence: _____
_____
_____
Source: _____

Fact: _____
Evidence: _____
_____
_____
Source: _____

Fact: _____
Evidence: _____
_____
_____
Source: _____

Conclusion: _____
_____
_____
_____
_____
_____
_____

# BIOGRAPHY RESEARCH

Biography of:

This person is known for:

Picture

Early life:

Famous Quote:

Important life events:

Accomplishments

Fun facts:

# PARTS OF THE BODY
### Answer Key
Label the body parts in this diagram.

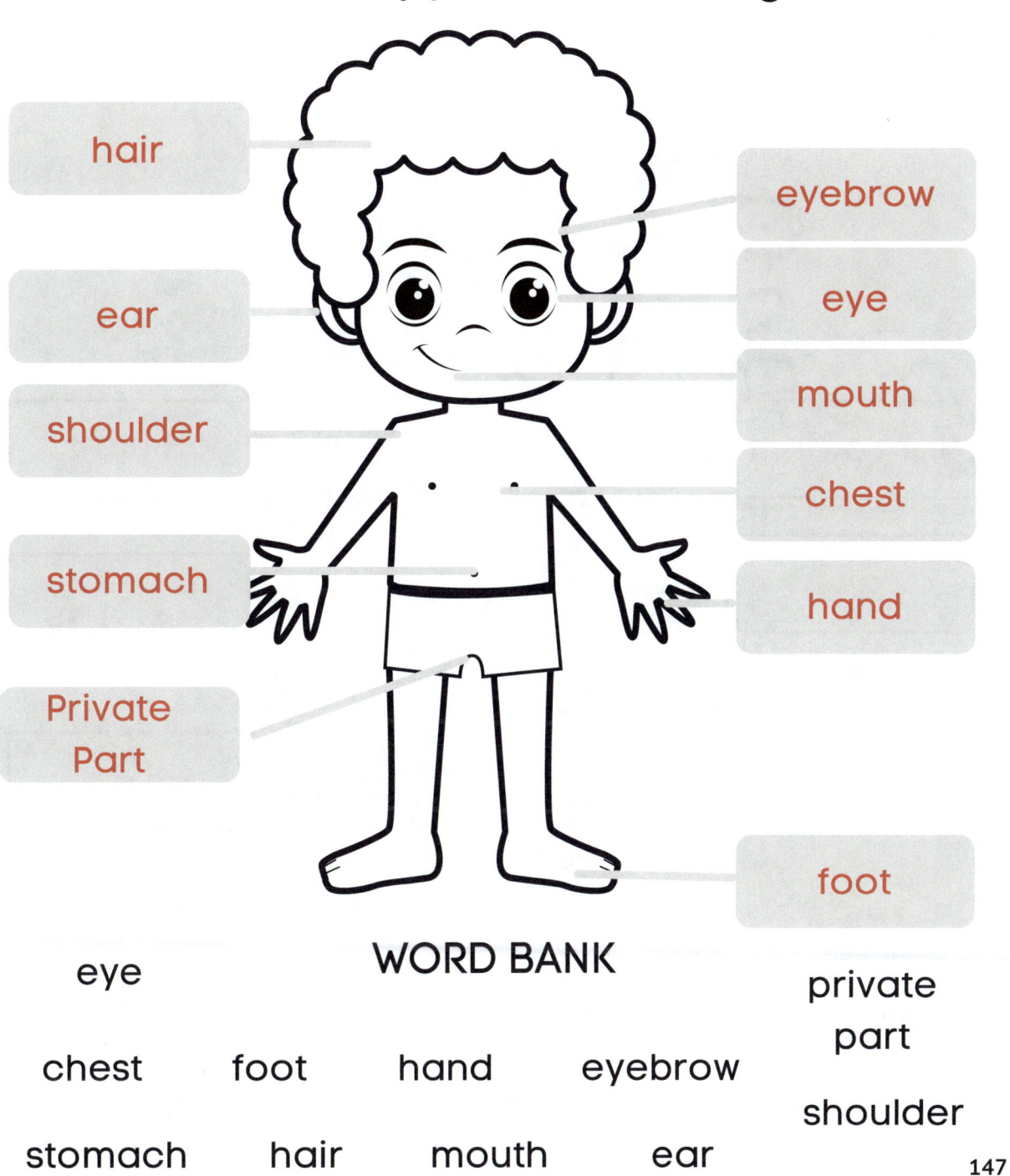

- hair
- ear
- shoulder
- stomach
- Private Part
- eyebrow
- eye
- mouth
- chest
- hand
- foot

## WORD BANK

eye  chest  foot  hand  eyebrow  private part  shoulder  stomach  hair  mouth  ear

147

# PARTS OF THE HEART

Answer Key

Label the parts of the heart.

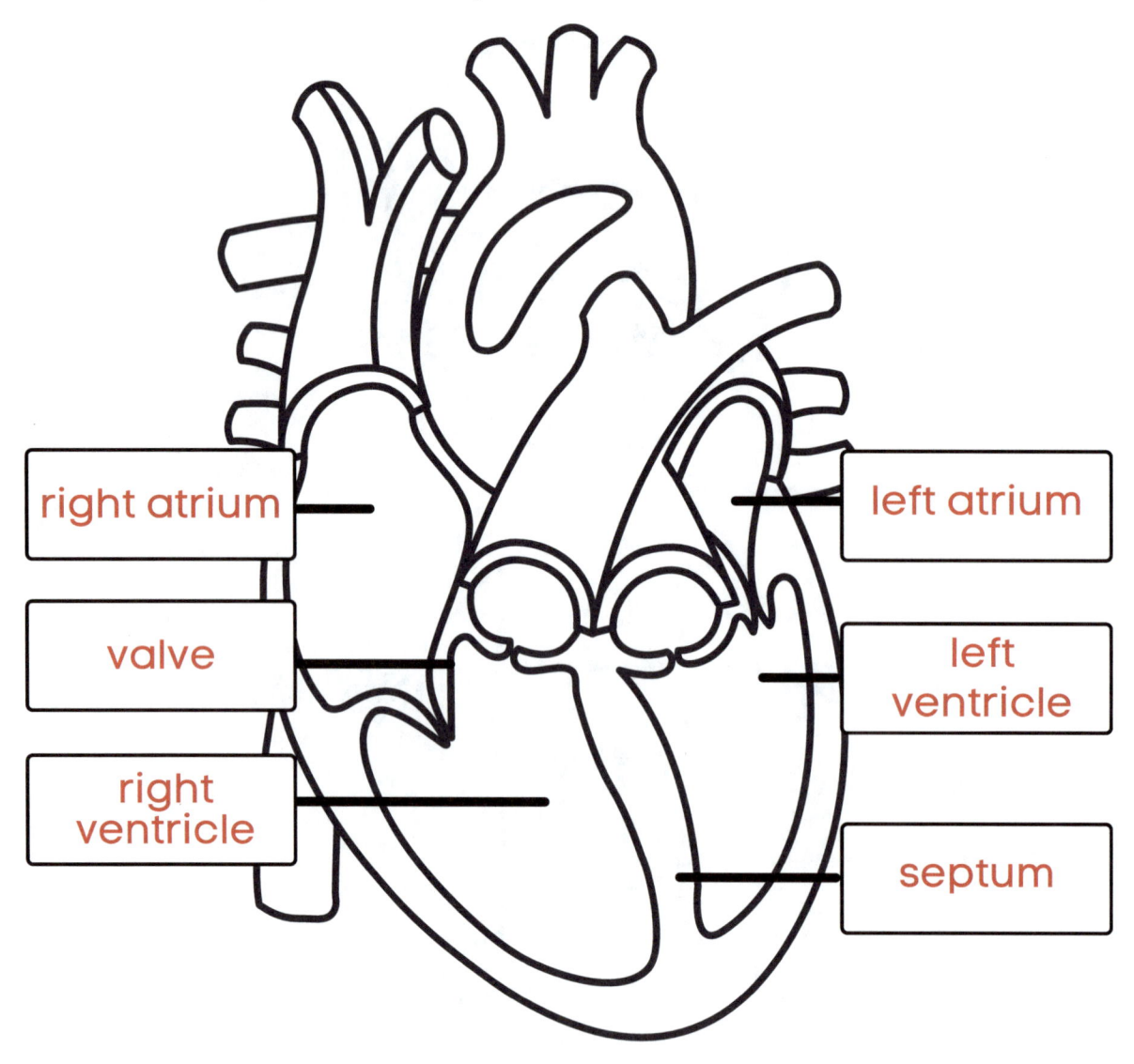

- right atrium
- valve
- right ventricle
- left atrium
- left ventricle
- septum

**WORD BANK**

| valve | left atrium | left ventricle |
| right atrium | septum | right ventricle |

# Answer Key

Below is an example of correct photosynthesis and cellular respiration. Students should use the elements appropriately, regardless of the flow.

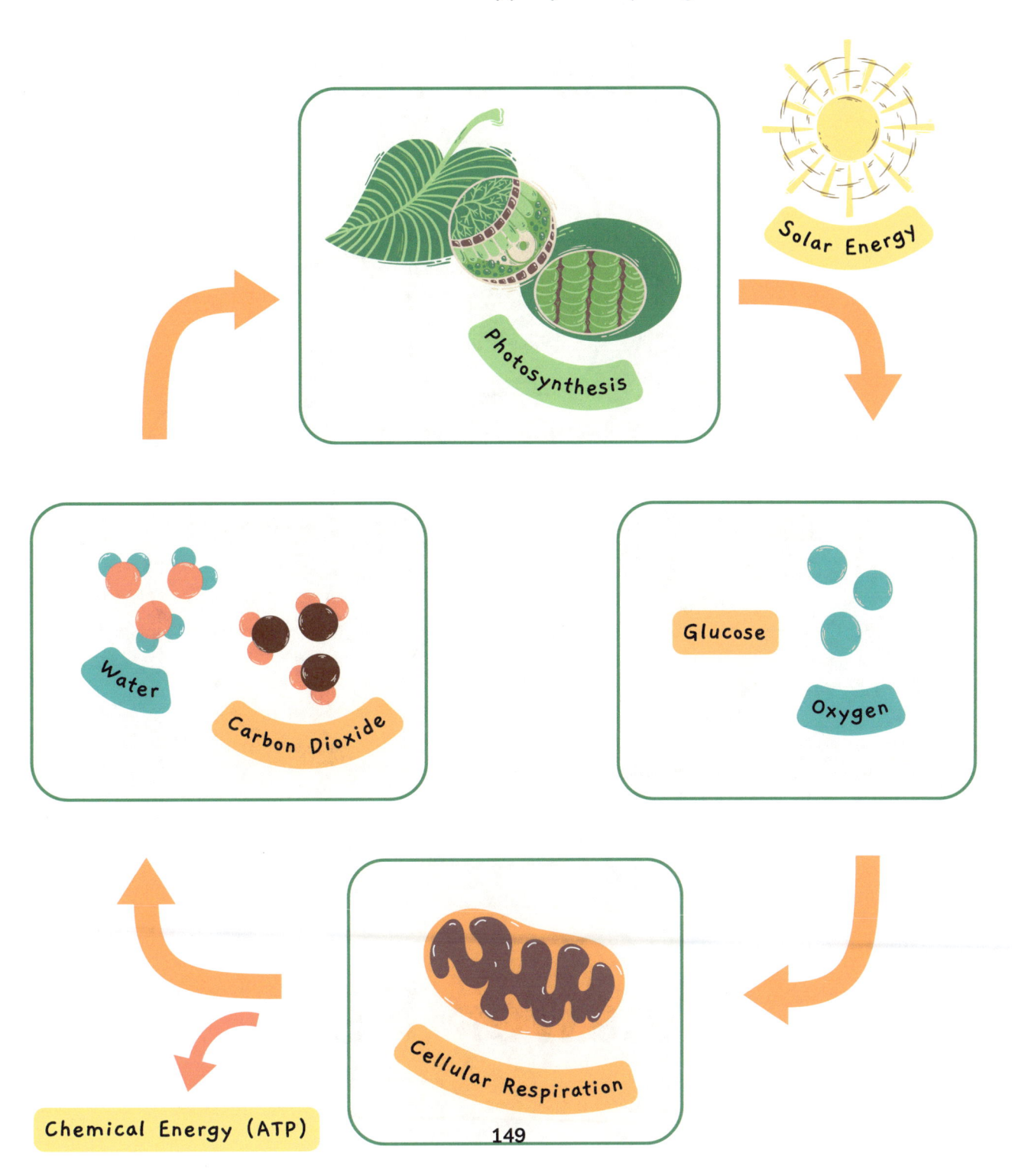

Solar Energy

Photosynthesis

Water

Carbon Dioxide

Glucose

Oxygen

Cellular Respiration

Chemical Energy (ATP)

# BUTTERFLY
## Life Cycle

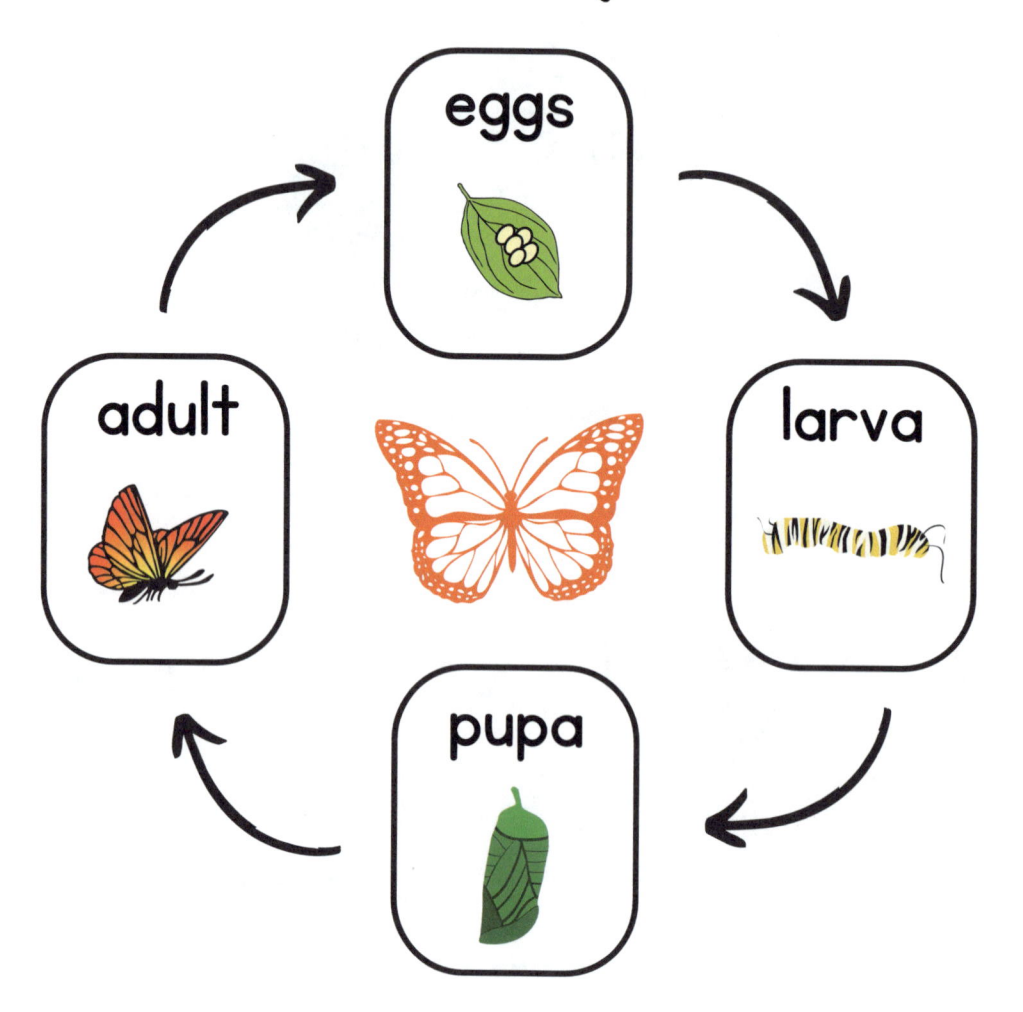

- eggs
- larva
- pupa
- adult

## Answer Key

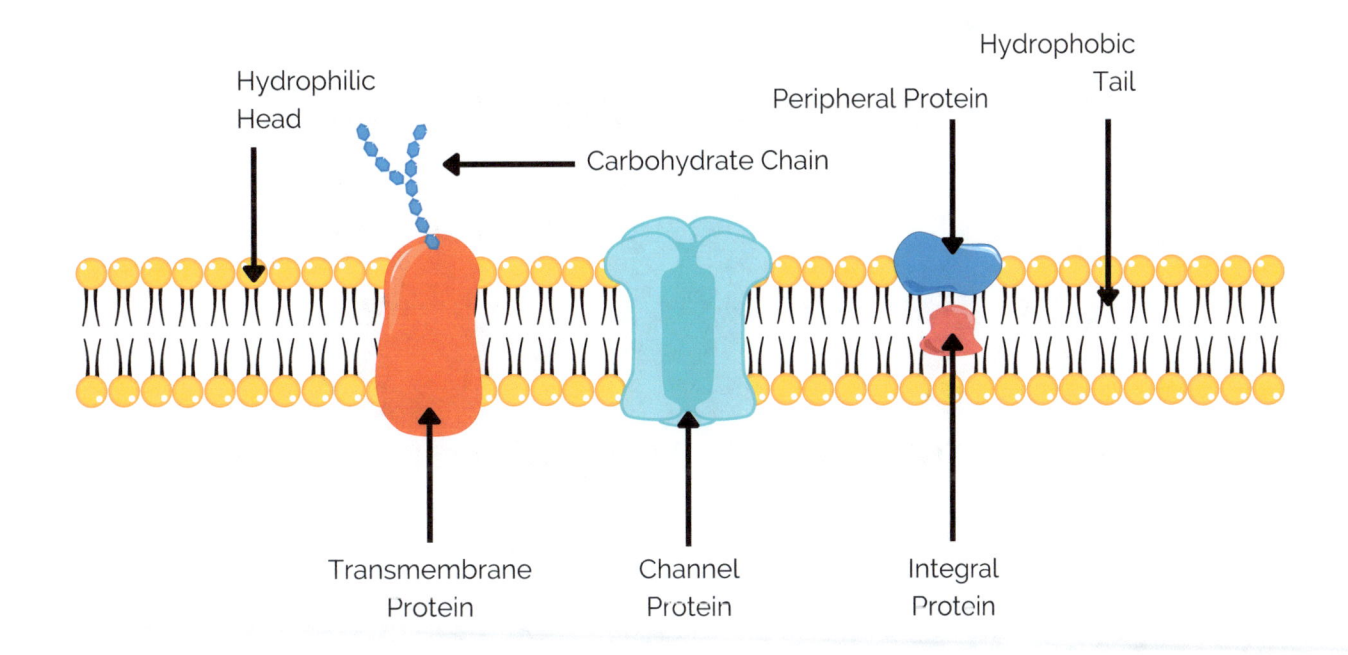

Answer Key

# THE CELL MEMBRANE

Directions: Use the terms below to label the parts of the cell membrane.

---

Transmembrane Protein        Channel Protein

Hydrophilic Head        Hydrophobic Tail        Peripheral Protein

Integral Protein        Carbohydrate Chain

---

Hydrophilic Head

Carbohydrate Chain

Peripheral Protein

Hydrophobic Tail

Transmembrane Protein

Channel Protein

Integral Protein

# CHANGES IN STATES OF MATTER
## Answer Key

Part I: Draw a line to match the change in state with its description.

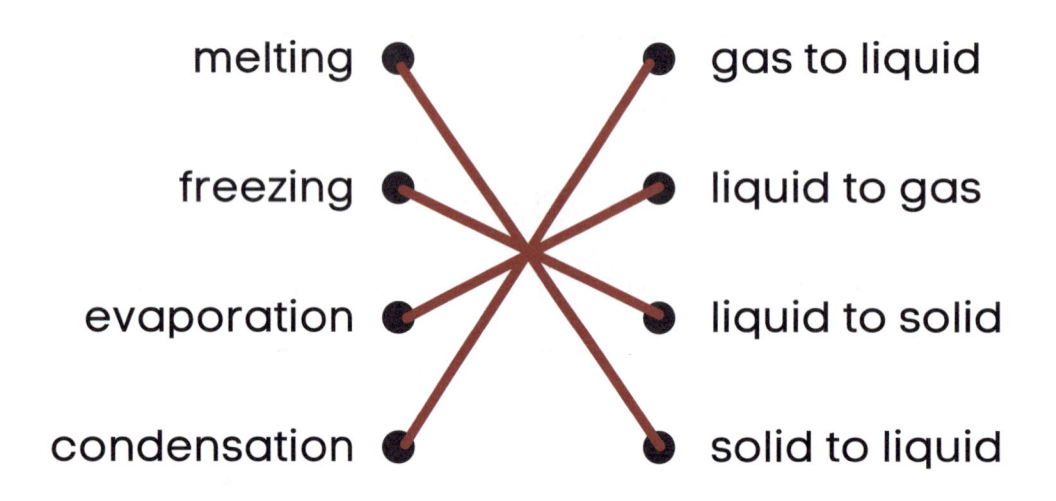

- melting — solid to liquid
- freezing — liquid to solid
- evaporation — liquid to gas
- condensation — gas to liquid

Part II: Label the following changes in state.

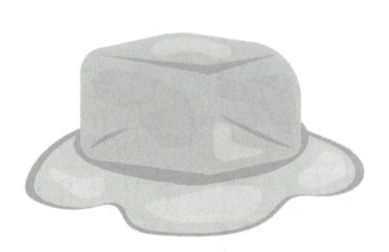

ice cube left out
**melting**

juice placed in a freezer
**freezing**

drying laundry
**evaporation**

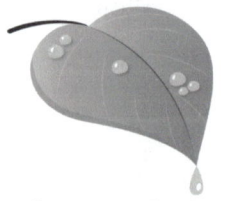

formation of dew drops
**condensation**

# CHANGES IN STATES OF MATTER

**Answer Key**

Complete the drawings below to represent changes in states of matter.

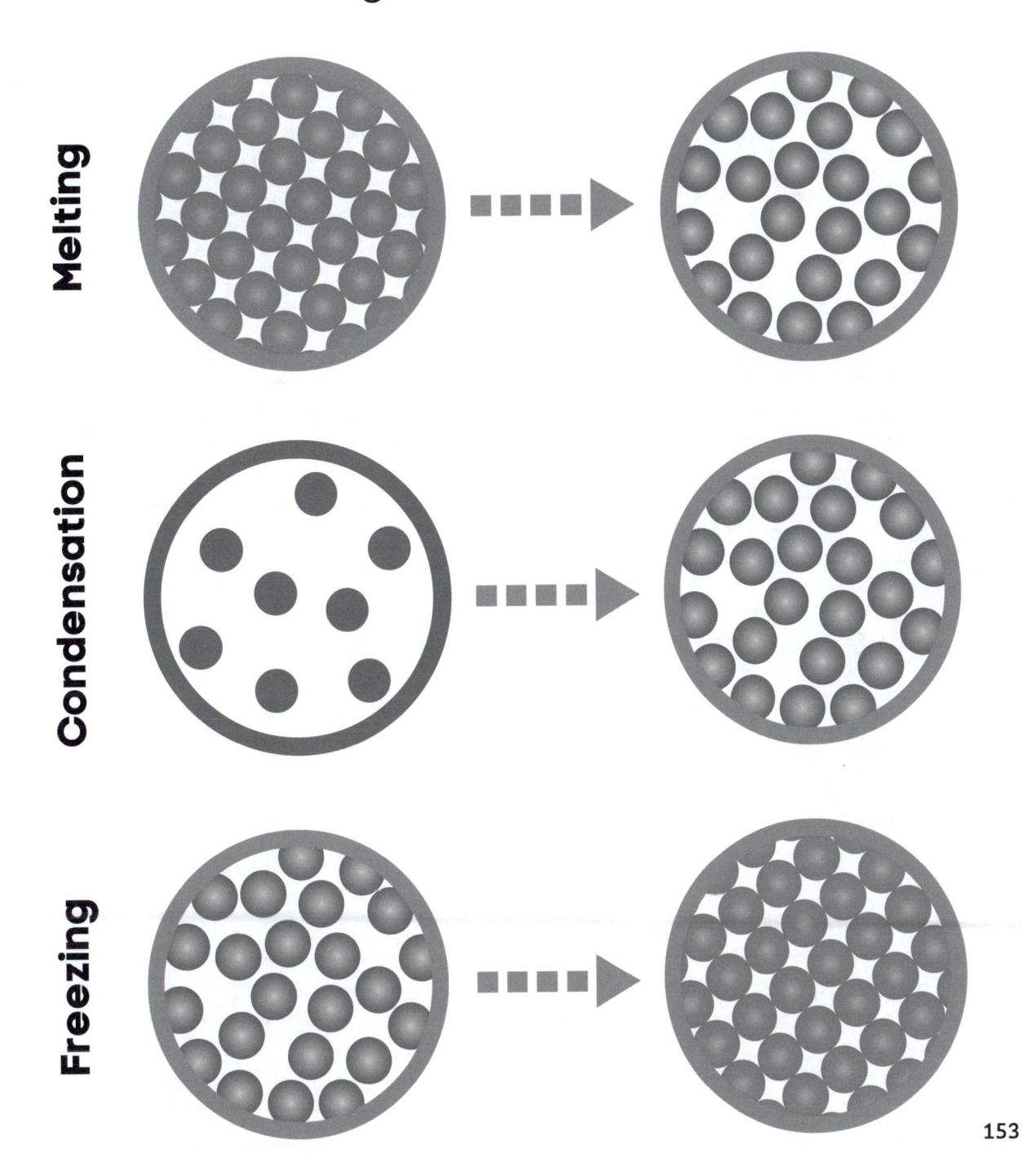

**Melting**

**Condensation**

**Freezing**

# STATES OF MATTER
### Answer Key
Describe the arrangement of atoms in each of the following state.

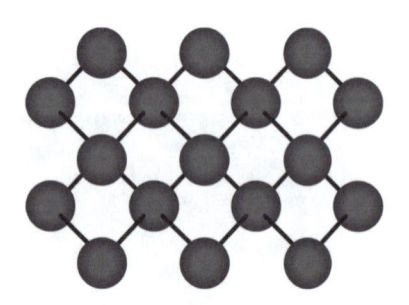

**solid**

The atoms in a solid are packed closely together.

**liquid**

The atoms in a liquid move more freely than those in solid.

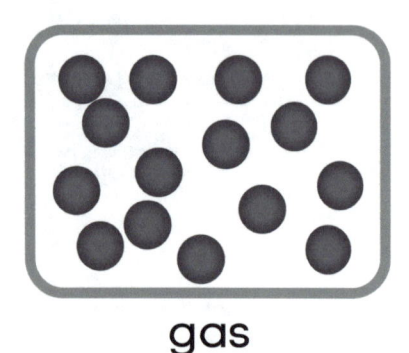

**gas**

The atoms in a gas are far apart. They move quickly.

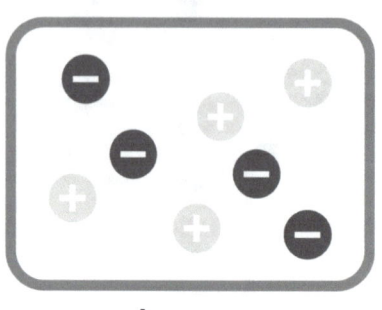

**plasma**

The atoms in a plasma are far apart. They are highly energetic.

# Additional Resources by A & W Publishing, LLC
## Available online!

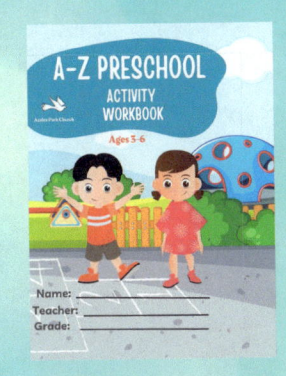

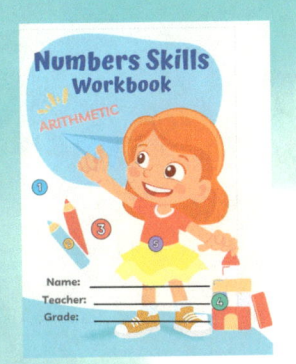

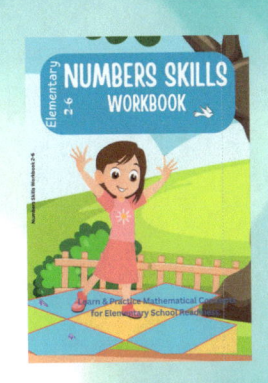

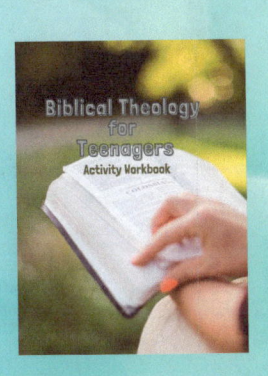

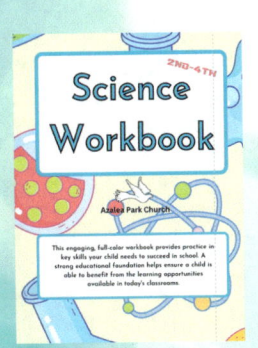

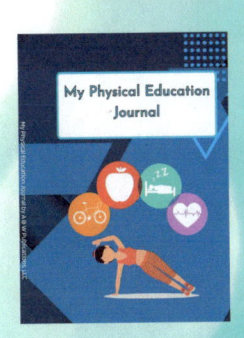

Made in the USA
Columbia, SC
08 August 2024